S0-BMZ-961

G. Allen Fleece Library
COLUMBIA INTERNATIONAL UNIVERSITY
7435 Monticello Road
Columbia, SC 29230

New Testament
Introduction

BIBLIOGRAPHIES

Tremper Longman III
General Editor and Old Testament Editor

Craig A. Evans
New Testament Editor

1. Pentateuch
2. Historical Books
3. Poetry and Wisdom
4. Prophecy and Apocalyptic
5. Jesus
6. Synoptic Gospels
7. Johannine Writings
8. Luke–Acts
9. Pauline Writings
10. Hebrews and General Epistles
11. Old Testament Introduction
12. New Testament Introduction
13. Old Testament Theology
14. New Testament Theology

New Testament Introduction

Stanley E. Porter
and
Lee M. McDonald

L P 494   441

 Baker Books

A Division of Baker Book House Co
Grand Rapids, Michigan 49516

© 1995 by Stanley E. Porter and Lee M. McDonald

Published by Baker Books
a division of Baker Book House Company
P.O. Box 6287, Grand Rapids, MI 49516-6287

Printed in the United States of America

All rights reserved. No part of this publication may be reproduced, stored in a retrieval system, or transmitted in any form or by any means—for example, electronic, photocopy, recording—without the prior written permission of the publisher. The only exception is brief quotations in printed reviews.

Library of Congress Cataloging-in-Publication Data

Porter, Stanley E., 1956–
    New Testament introduction / Stanley E. Porter and Lee McDonald.
       p.   cm. — (IBR bibliographies ; 12)
    ISBN 0-8010-2060-3
    1. Bible. N.T.—Introductions—Bibliography. I. McDonald, Lee
Martin, 1942–   . II. Title. III. Series: IBR bibliographies ; no. 12.
Z7772.L1P67   1995
[BS1140.2]
016.225—dc20   95-25608

Contents

Series Preface

With the proliferation of journals and publishing houses dedicated to biblical studies, it has become difficult for even the most dedicated scholar to keep in touch with the vast materials now available for research in the different parts of the canon. How much more challenging for the minister, rabbi, student, or interested layperson! Herein lies the importance of bibliographies and in particular this series—IBR Bibliographies.

Bibliographies help direct students to works that are relevant to their research interests. Bibliographies cut down the time needed to locate materials, thus providing the researcher with more time to read, assimilate, and write. These benefits are especially true for the IBR Bibliographies. First, the series is conveniently laid out along the major divisions of the canon, with four volumes planned on the Old Testament, six on the New Testament, and four on methodology (see page 2). Each volume will contain approximately five hundred entries, arranged under various topics to allow for ease of reference. Since the possible entries far exceed this number, the compiler of each volume must select the more important and helpful works for inclusion. Furthermore, the entries are briefly annotated in order to inform the reader about their contents more specifically, once again giving guidance to the appropriate material and saving time by preventing the all too typical "wild goose chase" in the library.

One of the problems with published bibliographies in the past is that they are soon out of date. The development of computer-based publishing has changed this, however, and it is the plan of the Institute for Biblical Research and Baker Book House to publish updates of each volume about every five years.

Since the series is designed primarily for American and British students, the emphasis is on works written in English, with a five-percent limit on titles not translated into English. Fortunately, a number of the most important foreign-language works have been translated into English, and wherever this is the case this information is included along with the original publication data. Again keeping in mind the needs of the student, we have decided to list the English translation before the original title (for chronological purposes, the titles are arranged according to the dates of their original publication).

These bibliographies are presented under the sponsorship of the Institute for Biblical Research (IBR), an organization of evangelical Christian scholars with specialties in both Old and New Testaments and their ancillary disciplines. The IBR has met annually since 1970; its name and constitution were adopted in 1973. Besides its annual meetings (normally held the evening and morning prior to the annual meeting of the Society of Biblical Literature), the institute publishes a journal, *Bulletin for Biblical Research,* and conducts regional study groups on various biblical themes in several areas of the United States and Canada. The Institute for Biblical Research encourages and fosters scholarly research among its members, all of whom are at a level to qualify for a university lectureship. Finally, the IBR and the series editor extend their thanks to Baker Book House for its efforts to bring this series to publication. In particular, we would like to thank David Aiken for his wise guidance in giving shape to the project.

Tremper Longman III
Westminster Theological Seminary

Authors' Preface

The primary problem of any bibliography—and one that we as authors of this one are acutely aware of—is that it is out of date at the moment of publication. This one is no exception. We have made every effort to be as current as the exigencies of publishing would allow. However, we have not sought to list the latest material only for its own sake. The secondary problem of any bibliography—and we are more than aware of this one as well—is that a bibliography often does not list the very work that one is seeking. We have not made an effort to list every work, as if that were a desirable or even a possible task. Far from it. Readers will notice that we have included a range of material, including older works that retain their value alongside newer works that bring discussion up to date. Our guiding principle is that we have tried to list and comment upon the wide range of works that would be the most helpful to students and scholars approaching a given topic, with enough introductory and advanced material to provide suitable guidance into the subject. We have complemented each other's work because of our contrasting and yet compatible interests, with the result that it is not desirable or feasible to try to single out which areas a given author has taken responsibility for. This has indeed been a project of joint authorship from start to finish. So much so in fact that we would like to thank two additional people in particular. Lee McDonald wishes to thank Kimlyn Bender for useful library and research work checking titles and bibliographic information. Stanley Porter wishes to thank his wife, Wendy, for her seemingly endless hours at the computer keyboard and the many trips into the British Library.

Abbreviations

AB	Anchor Bible
ABRL	Anchor Bible Reference Library
ALGHJ	Arbeiten zur Literatur und Geschichte des hellenistischen Judentums
ANRW	*Aufstieg und Niedergang der römischen Welt*
BETL	Bibliotheca ephemeridum theologicarum lovaniensium
BIS	Biblical Interpretation Series
BMT	The Bible and its Modern Interpreters
CBET	Contributors to Biblical Exegesis and Theology
CBQ	*Catholic Biblical Quarterly*
CC	Cambridge Commentaries and Writings of the Jewish and Christian World 200 B.C. to A.D. 200
CRINT	Compendium Rerum Iudaicarum ad Novum Testamentum
ExpTim	*Expository Times*
FCI	Foundations of Contemporary Interpretation
FF	Foundations and Facets
FN	*Filología Neotestamentaria*
FRLANT	Forschungen zur Religion und Literatur des Alten und Neuen Testaments
GBS	Guides to Biblical Scholarship
GNS	Good News Studies
HTR	*Harvard Theological Review*
HUT	Hermeneutische Untersuchungen zur Theologie
ICC	International Critical Commentary
JBL	*Journal of Biblical Literature*
JBLMS	Journal of Biblical Literature Monograph Series

JSNTSup	Journal for the Study of the New Testament Supplement Series
JSPSup	Journal for the Study of the Pseudepigrapha Supplement Series
LCL	Loeb Classical Library
LEC	Library of Early Christianity
MeyerK	H.A.W. Meyer (ed.), Kritisch-exegetischer Kommentar über das Neue Testament
NCB	New Century Bible
NICNT	New International Commentary on the New Testament
NIGTC	New International Greek Testament Commentary
NovTSup	Novum Testamentum Supplement Series
NTOA	Novum Testamentum et Orbis Antiquus
NTTS	New Testament Tools and Studies
OBS	Oxford Bible Series
OTM	Oxford Theological Monographs
SBG	Studies in Biblical Greek
SBLDS	Society of Biblical Literature Dissertation Series
SBLMS	Society of Biblical Literature Monograph Series
SBLRBS	Society of Biblical Literature Resources for Biblical Study
SBLSBS	Society of Biblical Literature Sources for Biblical Study
SBLSS	Society of Biblical Literature Scholarship Series
SBT	Studies in Biblical Theology
SCHNT	Studia ad Corpus Hellenisticum Novi Testamenti
SD	Studies and Documents
SJLA	Studies in Judaism in Late Antiquity
SNTSMS	Society for New Testament Studies Monograph Series
SP	Sacra Pagina
SSEJC	Studies in Scripture in Early Judaism and Christianity
TynBul	*Tyndale Bulletin*
UBSGNT	*United Bible Societies* Greek New Testament
WBC	Word Biblical Commentary
WUNT	Wissenschaftliche Untersuchungen zum Neuen Testament

Part 1

Interpretation Skills and Language

1

Exegetical Method

Exegesis as a discipline is under severe scrutiny. There is much rethinking of what constitutes exegesis, especially by those who advocate some of the newer interpretive methods. Although traditional exegesis could probably stand for some increase in perspectival flexibility, it is difficult to imagine convincing and enduring readings of ancient documents that do not consider at least the language of the text and the context in which the language is used. The most convincing discussions of exegetical method treat at least these two issues as fundamental, although they may include others as well, such as theology. Included below are (1) handbooks on exegesis for introductory perspectives and (2) several of the more recent volumes dedicated to describing and discussing critical method or volumes dedicated to discussing critical issues. A few of these latter volumes are written by single individuals but more typically these volumes are collections of essays, some of which could well be listed elsewhere in this volume as well. Not all of these volumes are equally effective, although the good ones may well be as good if not better than the single author handbooks.

1.1 Handbooks on Exegesis

1   H. Conzelmann and A. Lindemann. *Interpreting the New Testament: An Introduction to the Principles and Methods*

of New Testament Exegesis. Translated by S. S. Schatz-mann. Peabody: Hendrickson, 1988. Original title: *Arbeits-buch zum Neuen Testament.* Tübingen: Mohr-Siebeck. Eighth edition: 1985.

Arguably the best introduction to interpreting the New Testament. Although at almost every turn there is too lit-tle discussion, and probably not as much recognition of the non-German sources as one would want, there is a lit-tle something on most traditional areas of New Testa-ment interpretation. Most of the newer methods, how-ever, are not mentioned (that's why you have this book).

2   G. D. Fee. *New Testament Exegesis: A Handbook for Stu-dents and Pastors.* Philadelphia: Westminster, 1983. Second edition: Louisville: Westminster/John Knox/Leominster: Gracewing, 1993.

Fee's genre approach applied to exegesis for those with minimal Greek. It begins with grammar and ends with the sermon. There is useful bibliography, although much of it is not as current as it should be.

3   G. D. Fee and D. Stuart. *How to Read the Bible for All its Worth: A Guide to Understanding the Bible.* Grand Rapids: Zondervan, 1981. Second edition: 1993.

A generic approach to interpretation. Pretty basic stuff, especially since it does not put any stress on knowledge of the biblical languages.

4   J. H. Hayes and C. R. Holladay. *Biblical Exegesis: A Begin-ner's Handbook.* Atlanta: John Knox/London: SCM, 1982. Second edition: 1987.

A helpful guide to exegesis, in that it recognizes the vari-ous criticisms. The book is up to date enough to include literary criticism, besides the standards (textual, form, etc.). Basic bibliography is included.

5   O. Kaiser and W. G. Kümmel. *Exegetical Method: A Stu-dent's Handbook.* Translated by E. V. N. Goetchius and M. J. O'Connell. New York: Seabury, 1967. Second edition: 1981. Original publication: Munich: Kaiser, 1975.

A model of traditional higher-critical exegesis, that is, with no attention to recent methods. This is not necessarily a fault.

6   W. C. Kaiser, Jr. *Toward an Exegetical Theology: Biblical Exegesis for Preaching and Teaching.* Grand Rapids: Baker, 1981.

Kaiser's naive single intention hermeneutics comes through clearly. Although his idea of reading timeless principles off of a grammatical outline is an interesting one, it clearly doesn't work, as his example of 1 Thess. 4:1–8 teaching "Knowing the Will of God in Dating" clearly shows. Simplistic exegesis for the simple minded.

7   D. Lührmann. *An Itinerary for New Testament Study*. Philadelphia: Trinity Press International/London: SCM, 1989. Original title: *Auslegung des Neuen Testaments*. Zürich: Theologischer Verlag, 1984.

Divided into three parts—New Testament, historical theology, theological exegesis—the section on exegesis proper is incredibly brief. The emphasis makes it look like theology is the reason for exegesis. But how does one do theology on an inadequate exegetical foundation?

8   R. A. Muller. *Dictionary of Latin and Greek Theological Terms: Drawn Principally from Protestant Scholastic Theology.* Grand Rapids: Baker, 1985.

A most useful tool that gives in many instances detailed summaries of the meaning and use of key theological terms that are common *lingua franca* in biblical interpretation. Not exhaustive, but very informative.

9   R. N. Soulen. *Handbook of Biblical Criticism.* Atlanta: John Knox, 1976.

A veritable gold mine for students of the critical disciplines of New Testament inquiry. Loaded with helpful definitions and brief explanations of terms, phrases, names, and disciplines employed in New Testament interpretation and a collection of some 60 individuals who play a major role in the field. Downright practical.

10   W. Stenger. *Introduction to New Testament Exegesis.* Translated by D. W. Stott. Grand Rapids: Eerdmans, 1993.

Original title: *Biblische Methodenlehre*. Düsseldorf: Patmos, 1987.

Brief introduction to the practice of exegesis, emphasizing diachronic method but weak on language. Attempts to demonstrate the method on ten passages from the New Testament. Preaching the text is in mind.

11 W. R. Tate. *Biblical Interpretation: An Integrated Approach*. Peabody: Hendrickson, 1991.

Usefully divides critical approaches into author-, text- and reader-centered methods, with most sympathy for text-centered. Reflects orientation of some earlier literary critics (e.g., M. Abrams).

12 N. Turner. *Handbook for Biblical Studies*. Philadelphia: Westminster, 1982.

Useful guide to the scholarly jargon of biblical interpretation. Some 1500 entries.

1.2 Discussions of Critical Method

13 D. A. Black and D. S. Dockery (eds.). *New Testament Criticism and Interpretation*. Grand Rapids: Zondervan, 1991.

A collected volume on New Testament interpretation. Many essays, and a few good ones, such as textual criticism by M. W. Holmes (pp. 101–34), source criticism by S. McKnight (pp. 137–72), canonical criticism by M. C. Parsons (pp. 255–94), and literary genres by C. L. Blomberg (pp. 507–32). To be avoided are essays on literary criticism and Greek grammar.

14 D. A. Carson. *Exegetical Fallacies*. Grand Rapids: Baker, 1984.

An excellent book at deflating a lot of bad exegetical practice. Carson notes mistakes in four areas, including lexicography, grammar, logic, and historical method.

15 E. J. Epp and G. W. MacRae (eds.). *The New Testament and its Modern Interpreters*. Atlanta: Scholars Press, 1989.

A varied collection in all ways, in terms of quality, timeliness (the book was severely delayed), and bibliography. Nevertheless, there is much worth consulting here for potted summaries of virtually all of the major areas of

New Testament interpretation, usually written by experts in the fields. Lengthy bibliographies.

16 K. Froehlich (trans. and ed.). *Biblical Interpretation in the Early Church.* Sources of Early Christian Thought. Philadelphia: Fortress, 1984.

A small but significant work that focuses on the kinds of interpretation that circulated in the ancient Jewish and Christian communities. Most of the illustrations are from the patristic period, but they all tie into the use of the biblical text.

17 A. E. Harvey (ed.). *Alternative Approaches to New Testament Study.* London: SPCK, 1985.

A mixed collection of essays, proposing new directions using the traditional critical methods. One of the outstanding contributions is M. Goulder's now well-known "A House Built on Sand" (pp. 1–24), in which he argues for dispensing with Q.

18 G. F. Hawthorne with O. Betz (eds.). *Tradition and Interpretation in the New Testament: Essays in Honor of E. E. Ellis for his 60th Birthday.* Grand Rapids: Eerdmans/Tübingen: Mohr-Siebeck, 1987.

Several significant introductory essays in this Festschrift volume include I. H. Marshall disputing with E. Käsemann that apocalyptic is the mother of Christian theology (pp. 33–41), C. F. D. Moule reexamining the relation between Jesus, Judaism, and Paul and finding E. P. Sanders not entirely convincing (pp. 43–52), and D. M. Smith raising significant questions of canon (pp. 166–80), among many others.

19 G. E. Ladd. *The New Testament and Criticism.* Grand Rapids: Eerdmans, 1967.

Concise conservative comments on the major areas of New Testament criticism, including textual criticism, linguistic criticism, literary criticism, form criticism, historical criticism, and comparative religions criticism. Not much documentation but reasonable introductions to the subjects.

20   R. N. Longenecker and M. C. Tenney (eds.). *New Dimensions in New Testament Study.* Grand Rapids: Zondervan, 1974.

This excellent collection of essays has a number of significant contributions in the area of introduction by F. F. Bruce on the canon (pp. 3–18), G. D. Fee on p66 and p75 (pp. 19–45), E. M. Yamauchi on gnosticism (pp. 46–70), R. H. Gundry on the genre "Gospel" (pp. 97–114), P. E. Hughes on the language of Jesus (pp. 127–43), and Longenecker on amanuenses and the Pauline epistles (pp. 281–97).

21   S. McKnight (ed.). *Introducing New Testament Interpretation.* Guides to New Testament Exegesis. Grand Rapids: Baker, 1989.

Several of the essays are worth reading, including M. W. Holmes on textual criticism (pp. 53–74), T. E. Schmidt on sociology and New Testament exegesis (pp. 115–32), L. D. Hurst on theology (pp. 133–61), and C. A. Evans on the use of the Old Testament (pp. 163–93).

22   I. H. Marshall (ed.). *New Testament Interpretation: Essays on Principles and Methods.* Grand Rapids: Eerdmans/Exeter: Paternoster, 1977.

Several of the essays in this volume covering the major areas of New Testament interpretation have become classics, including A. C. Thiselton's "Semantics and New Testament Interpretation" (pp. 75–104) and "The New Hermeneutic" (pp. 308–33). Also very useful are G. N. Stanton on presuppositions in New Testament criticism (pp. 60–72) and D. R. Catchpole on tradition history (pp. 165–80). Other contributors include F. F. Bruce, I. H. Marshall, R. T. France, D. Wenham, S. Travis, and J. D. G. Dunn. Still the best book of its kind.

23   H. Palmer. *The Logic of Gospel Criticism: An Account of the Methods and Arguments Used by Textual, Documentary, Source, and Form Critics of the New Testament.* New York: St. Martin's/London: Macmillan, 1968.

Insightful and iconoclastic study that subjects methods and argumentation used by New Testament scholars to necessary close scrutiny. Many times the methods of New Testament criticism do not come across as particularly well-informed, logical, or rigorous.

24 C. Tuckett. *Reading the New Testament: Methods of Interpretation.* London: SPCK, 1987.

Useful survey of the various critical methods. Most time is spent on the traditional historical-critical methods, which come off best in his treatment, in which he lumps such things as literary criticism and canonical criticism into one category. His chapter on sociology is succinct and helpful.

2

Hermeneutics

The field of hermeneutics has changed radically within the last twenty years. What used to be a field concerned with identifying figures of speech and literary genres has become recognizably highly complex. The modern discussion of hermeneutics includes difficult questions about the nature and function of language, what it means for language to refer, the meaning of "meaning," the problem in arriving at universal statements from contingent documents, the bridging of the horizons of text and reader, the history of how texts have been interpreted and the effect that various interpretations have had on their receiving communities, to name only a few. One interested in hermeneutics will probably want to read widely in general philosophy, philosophy of language, and philosophy of history. Specialized texts in these areas are not included below.

25 V. Brümmer. *Theology and Philosophical Inquiry: An Introduction.* Philadelphia: Westminster, 1982.

An excellent introduction to many of the basic philosophical questions that apply to doing theology.

2.1 Basic Works in Hermeneutics

26 R. J. Coggins and J. L. Houlden (eds.). *A Dictionary of Biblical Interpretation.* Philadelphia: Trinity Press International/London: SCM, 1990.

A handy volume, in that topics that biblical scholars confront are addressed from an interpretive framework. Some of the essays are very good, although occasionally it is difficult to know why certain contributors were selected. Many contemporary topics are covered (e.g., intertextuality, linguistics) but a few rather important other topics are missed (e.g., Greek, Hebrew, Aramaic, although Aramaisms and Semitisms have their own entries).

27 D. K. McKim (ed.). *A Guide to Contemporary Hermeneutics: Major Trends in Biblical Interpretation.* Grand Rapids: Eerdmans, 1986.

A reasonable survey of the subject by means of excerpts from primary sources. This provides an ideal reader as a quick entry point and as a supplement to discussion.

28 W. W. Klein, C. L. Blomberg, and R. L. Hubbard, with K. A. Ecklebarger. *Introduction to Biblical Interpretation.* Dallas: Word, 1992.

A conservative introduction to interpretation seen as exegesis. Attention is paid to matters of language and genre. Much of the research is up to date but interpretations are sometimes questionable, e.g., the discussion on canon.

29 G. R. Osborne. *The Hermeneutical Spiral: A Comprehensive Introduction to Biblical Interpretation.* Downers Grove: InterVarsity, 1991.

A huge book, virtually unusable as a textbook, although it might fare better as a reference volume. It combines many of the traditional questions of hermeneutics with at least a recognition of the more complex philosophical and related issues. Osborne tends to take the middle road, opting for inclusion rather than exclusion, resulting in some interesting anomalies and potential contradictions. Essentially every topic is mentioned at one place or another.

30 E. C. Blackman. *Biblical Interpretation.* Philadelphia: Westminster/London: Independent Press, 1957.

Still valuable for its concise summary of the development of interpretation.

31   R. Bultmann. *Existence and Faith: The Shorter Writings of R. Bultmann.* Translated by S. Ogden. New York/London: Meridian, 1960.

   Included in this collection is Bultmann's classic "Is Exegesis without Presuppositions Possible?" (pp. 342–51).

32   W. C. Kaiser, Jr. and M. Silva. *Introduction to Biblical Hermeneutics: The Search for Meaning.* Grand Rapids: Zondervan, 1993.

   This is a difficult book to follow, especially Kaiser, but also Silva who appears to minimize the scholarship he employs in his investigation. Not as useful as other texts.

33   M. Silva. *Has the Church Misread the Bible? The History of Interpretation in the Light of Current Issues.* FCI 1. Grand Rapids: Zondervan/Leicester: InterVarsity, 1987.

   Raises many of the right questions but ducks many of the logical answers. Traditional grammatical-historical answers are offered in an unconvincing way.

34   V. Poythress. *Science and Hermeneutics: Implications of Scientific Method for Biblical Interpretation.* FCI 6. Grand Rapids: Zondervan/Leicester: InterVarsity, 1988.

   A struggle to come to terms with the influence of scientific method on biblical hermeneutics. The explanations are often given in a condescending tone. The appendix with bibliography is very useful.

35   R. G. Gruenler. *Meaning and Understanding: The Philosophical Framework for Biblical Interpretation.* FCI 2. Grand Rapids: Zondervan, 1991.

   A basic introduction, differentiating Continental and English-type philosophical schools.

2.2 Advanced Works in Hermeneutics

36   W. G. Jeanrond. *Text and Interpretation as Categories of Theological Thinking.* Translated by T. J. Wilson. New York: Crossroad/Dublin: Gill and Macmillan, 1988. Original title: *Text und Interpretation als Kategorien theologischen Denkens.* HUT 23. Tübingen: Mohr-Siebeck, 1986.

   Jeanrond appreciates the process of both production and reception of the text. While acknowledging the validity of categories such as reader-response, he places most emphasis upon text-linguistic analysis for establishing meaning. Modern linguistic categories are given their due.

37   W. G. Jeanrond. *Theological Hermeneutics: Development and Significance.* New York: Crossroad, 1991.

A brief history of hermeneutics, followed by a popularization of the ideas first developed in *Text and Interpretation* (see no. 36). Theology gets its due in Jeanrond's treatment.

38   D. Nineham. *The Use and Abuse of the Bible: A Study of the Bible in an Age of Rapid Cultural Change.* London: Macmillan, 1976.

For Nineham the distance between the age of the Bible and our own is so great that it makes objective interpretation of the Bible impossible.

39   P. Ricoeur. *Essays on Biblical Interpretation.* Edited by L. S. Mudge. Philadelphia: Fortress, 1980.

The heart of this book is four essays by Ricoeur that originally appeared in French in the 1960s and 1970s, supplemented by a discussion between the author and editor. The attempt is to mediate Ricoeur's thought on the Bible—which could be very important in biblical hermeneutics—directly to readers, rather than through his other works and other interpreters. One gets a sense of Ricoeur's literarily based structural-formalist interpretive stance. See also his *Interpretation Theory: Discourse and the Surplus of Meaning.* Fort Worth: Texas Christian University Press, 1976, and *Hermeneutics and the Human Sciences: Essays on Language, Action and Interpretation.* Translated and edited by J. B. Thompson. Cambridge: Cambridge University Press/Paris: Editions de la Maison des Sciences de l'Homme, 1981. For an analysis see K. Vanhoozer. *Biblical Narrative in the Philosophy of Paul Ricoeur: A Study in Hermeneutics and Theology.* Cambridge: Cambridge University Press, 1990.

40   A. C. Thiselton. *The Two Horizons: New Testament Hermeneutics and Philosophical Description with Special Reference to Heidegger, Bultmann, Gadamer, and Wittgenstein.* Grand Rapids: Eerdmans/Exeter: Paternoster, 1980.

A challenging and important description of these major
figures and their relevance for biblical studies, set within
the larger context of philosophical and theological
hermeneutics. Parts one and two are useful introductions
to the topics involved. Thiselton has established himself
as one of the most philosophically informed New Testament scholars. See no. 41 for the continuation volume.

41   A. C. Thiselton. *New Horizons in Hermeneutics: The Theory and Practice of Transforming Biblical Reading.* Grand
Rapids: Zondervan/London: HarperCollins, 1992.

A massive work, extending his *The Two Horizons* (see no.
40) by analyzing other significant figures in hermeneutics
and offering his own model of interpretive theory based
upon speech-act theory. One does not necessarily need to
agree with the analysis of others or the applicability of
speech-act theory to the interpretation of ancient documents to appreciate the important survey of work
amassed here.

42   R. Lundin, A. C. Thiselton, and C. Walhout. *The Responsibility of Hermeneutics.* Grand Rapids: Eerdmans/Exeter:
Paternoster, 1985.

These three authors each contribute about a third of the
volume. Lundin discusses the philosophical background
to modern hermeneutics, Walhout tries to get away from
a theory of literature as language to a theory of literature
as action (of course, he doesn't get away from using language to outline his theory), and Thiselton outlines his
model of speech-act theory and applies it to the parables
of Jesus.

43   R. W. Funk. *Language, Hermeneutic and Word of God: The
Problem of Language in the New Testament and Contemporary Theology.* New York: Harper & Row, 1966.

A highly influential work that brought the new hermeneutic to play in English-speaking circles. Also important
is his section on the letter form and style (pp. 250–74).

44   N. T. Wright. *The New Testament and the People of God.*
I. *Christian Origins and the Question of God.* London:
SPCK, 1992.

Well informed introductions to some crucial hermeneutical problems are too long even for New Testament scholars. Perhaps too easily concludes with a commonsensical answer to the set of issues.

45 P. Stuhlmacher. *Historical Criticism and Theological Interpretation of Scripture: Toward a Hermeneutics of Consent.* Translated by R. A. Harrisville. Philadelphia: Fortress/London: SPCK, 1977. Original title: "Historische Kritik und theologische Schriftauslegung" in *Schriftauslegung auf dem Wege zur biblischen Theologie.* Göttingen: Vandenhoeck & Ruprecht, 1975.

An important essay that attempts to find relevance for historical criticism by connecting it with theology. Stuhlmacher introduces a hermeneutics of consent, in which there is an openness to transcendence within the context of critical method. Carefully written and well-informed.

46 G. D. Fee. *Gospel and Spirit: Issues in New Testament Hermeneutics.* Peabody: Hendrickson, 1991.

Although Fee's hermeneutics may be a bit old fashioned for some, his addressing of issues that have divided evangelicals is welcome. His solutions, which freely run contrary to many of the establishment positions, are even more welcome.

47 J. S. Croatto. *Biblical Hermeneutics: Toward a Theory of Reading as the Production of Meaning.* Translated by R. R. Barr. Maryknoll: Orbis, 1987. Original title: *Hermenéutica bíblica: Para una teoría de la lectura como producción senido.* Buenos Aires: Asociación Ediciones la Aurora, 1984.

The title is descriptive of the approach. The author tries to make interpretation relevant. The approach is a bit skewed, since hermeneutics is seen as a particular approach concerned with modern relevance.

3

Greek Language, Linguistics, and Translation Theory

Many scholars are unaware of the considerable advances made in the study of Greek language in the last thirty years. The major progress has been made as modern linguistic methods have been applied to the study of Greek. This has caused many tried and true assumptions to be reexamined, sometimes to the consternation of those who have become very comfortable with what they have considered to be solid grammatical foundations for theological beliefs. The exegetes and commentary writers reflect an earlier period of discussion that depends heavily upon many of the older standard reference tools. Although a number of journals occasionally publish articles in the area of grammar, two journals have done considerable work recently. *Grace Theological Journal* in the 1980s and into the early 1990s ran a number of basic but useful articles. Unfortunately, the journal is no longer published. In 1988 a new journal, *Filología Neotestamentaria,* began publication. It is devoted to matters of language. Almost every issue has something of value.

3.1 Method

Study of the language of the New Testament marked by methodological awareness began with J. Barr (see no. 48). This is not to say that there was not competent and valuable study of Greek before 1961—far from the case—or that all study after Barr has been marked by methodological soundness. Unfortunately, there is much ill-informed study done by those who should know better. This section includes works that show awareness of the kinds of issues that modern linguistics raises for study of the Greek of the New Testament. Not all of these are successful, but the best ones provide useful guidelines for exegesis.

48   J. Barr. *The Semantics of Biblical Language*. Oxford: Oxford University Press, 1961.

   This is the classic study that put Kittel's lexicon (see no. 117) in its place, as well as helped to explode other unlinguistic myths about the languages of the Bible. Often referred to but still neglected, it is amazing to see how many of the issues that Barr clearly analyzed still prove to be difficulties for the uninformed and unenlightened, such as mischaracterizations of Greek and Hebrew. It's worth the price.

49   D. A. Black. *Linguistics for Students of New Testament Greek: A Survey of Basic Concepts and Applications*. Grand Rapids: Baker, 1988.

   A mixed bag of issues related to the study of Greek. The introduction of modern linguistics to second year Greek students is commendable, even though the various approaches utilized and explanations offered are not always convincing.

50   G. B. Caird. *The Language and Imagery of the Bible*. Philadelphia: Westminster/London: Duckworth, 1980.

   A common-sensical approach to linguistics. Although the book may be a bit naive and does go astray a few times (for example on the discussion of Hebrew idiom and thought), Caird at least has made an attempt to come to terms with issues of language in the study of the Bible.

51   P. Cotterell and M. Turner. *Linguistics and Biblical Interpretation*. Downers Grove: InterVarsity/London: SPCK, 1989.

   An eclectic attempt at a comprehensive introduction, using various linguistic methodologies. Some are informative, such as the criticism of Kittel and the sections on discourse analysis, while others are surprisingly unlinguistic, such as those on sentence clusters and nonliteral language. Linguistics is rightly seen as part of the hermeneutical enterprise. Overall perhaps the best introduction.

52   J. P. Louw. *Semantics of New Testament Greek*. Philadelphia: Fortress/Chico: Scholars Press, 1982.

One of the first treatments that made use of modern linguistic methodology in studying the Greek of the New Testament. The approach is a modified transformational grammar shared with many Bible Society translators. There are sections on lexis and grammar.

53   E. A. Nida. "The Implications of Contemporary Linguistics for Biblical Scholarship." *JBL* 91 (1972) 73–89.

One of the first articles to try to bridge the gap between traditional philologically-based (and usually outmoded) biblical studies and recent developments in modern linguistics. Although what is said may still seem new to many biblical scholars, much of the material is from a linguistic standpoint quite old hat.

54   S. E. Porter. "Studying Ancient Languages from a Modern Linguistic Perspective: Essential Terms and Terminology." *FN* 2 (1989) 147–72.

Introduction to the major issues raised by modern linguistics for the study of ancient languages, especially Greek. Many of the issues treated are not often discussed when Greek is discussed. Some of the implications of these issues for lexicography and syntax are treated in S. E. Porter. "Greek Language and Linguistics." *ExpTim* 103.7 (1992) 202–8.

55   M. Silva. *God, Language and Scripture: Reading the Bible in the Light of General Linguistics*. FCI 4. Grand Rapids: Zondervan/Leicester: InterVarsity, 1990.

An unconvincing book, since it overlooks recent works, and, in its shying away from new insights, helps to reconfirm ideas that are no longer tenable regarding the lack of importance of linguistics for the study of the New Testament.

3.2 Language of the New Testament

A long-standing debate concerns the nature of the Greek of the New Testament. The range of opinions has varied from a special Holy Ghost Greek, to being part and parcel of the common Greek of the day, to some form of mixed Greek. Recent work in bilingualism has pushed discussion forward by moving away from simply comparing isolated features of Aramaic or Hebrew and Greek. Most of the studies that have argued for strong Semitic influence on the Greek of the New Testament have been shown to be inadequate. Included in this section are histories of the Greek language, useful in establishing the larger context of development of hellenistic Greek, of which the Greek of the New Testament is a part.

56   M. Black. *An Aramaic Approach to the Gospels and Acts.* Oxford: Clarendon, 1946. Third edition: 1967.

   A still useful though dated summary of many of the issues regarding the Aramaic background to the New Testament. Black takes a moderate position, denying that the Gospels were originally written in Aramaic, but finding a good number of instances where (he thinks) Semitic background can explain difficult Greek.

57   P. W. Costas. *An Outline of the History of the Greek Language, with Particular Emphasis on the Koine and the Subsequent Periods.* Chicago: Ukrainian Society of Sciences of America, 1936. Reprinted Chicago: Ares, 1979.

   Still one of the best and most concise histories of Greek written in English.

58   R. Browning. *Medieval and Modern Greek.* Cambridge: Cambridge University Press, 1969. Second edition: 1983.

   An excellent brief history of the language, especially the first two chapters (pp. 19–52). Whereas many histories of the Greek language begin in the earliest periods and end with the hellenistic period, this book begins with the hellenistic period and works forward.

59 C. D. Buck. *The Greek Dialects: Grammar, Selected Inscriptions, Glossary.* Chicago: University of Chicago Press, 1955.

Still the standard treatment of the Greek dialects, with illustrative texts for examination.

60 E. C. Colwell. *The Greek of the Fourth Gospel: A Study of its Aramaisms in the Light of Hellenistic Greek.* Chicago: University of Chicago Press, 1931.

A defense of the Fourth Gospel against the charge of being written in Aramaisms, with useful examples from the papyri and other nonliterary hellenistic writers.

61 J. Doudna. *The Greek of the Gospel of Mark.* JBLMS 12. Philadelphia: Society of Biblical Literature and Exegesis, 1961.

A brief but well-documented analysis of the Greek of the Gospel of Mark, appreciating similarities to the nonliterary Greek of the time.

62 J. K. Elliott (ed.). *The Language and Style of the Gospel of Mark: An Edition of C. H. Turner's "Notes on Marcan Usage" together with Other Comparable Studies.* NovTSup 71. Leiden: Brill, 1993.

Reprinting of essays by C. H. Turner that appeared in *JTS* between 1924–28, plus eight essays by G. D. Kilpatrick (several published for the first time), two previously published essays by Elliott, and one chapter from N. Turner's *Style* (see no. 75) on Mark. This is a strange collection. C. H. Turner's essays are interesting but certainly dated now.

63 S. Lieberman. *Greek in Jewish Palestine: Studies in the Life and Manners of Jewish Palestine in the II-IV Centuries C.E.* New York: Feldheim, 1942. Second edition: 1965.

One of the first to recognize and clearly substantiate the Greek influence upon Palestinian Judaism, even in its language.

64 E. C. Maloney. *Semitic Interference in Marcan Syntax.* SBLDS 51. Chico: Scholars Press, 1981.

A fairly balanced analysis of possible Semitisms in Mark, with wider application to the New Testament a possibility. Maloney differentiates various levels of possible Semitic influence.

65 S. E. Porter. "Jesus and the Use of Greek in Galilee." Pp. 123–54 in *Studying the Historical Jesus: Evaluations of the State of Current Research.* Edited by B. Chilton and C. A. Evans. NTTS 19. Leiden: Brill, 1994.

A heavily annotated summary of the century-long discussion regarding which language Jesus used (Aramaic, Hebrew, or Greek), assuming that Jesus spoke Aramaic but arguing that the evidence for his knowledge of Greek is stronger than usually realized. See also S. E. Porter. "Did Jesus Ever Teach in Greek?" *TynBul* 44.2 (1993) 199–235.

66 S. E. Porter (ed.). *The Language of the New Testament: Classic Essays.* JSNTSup 60. Sheffield: JSOT Press, 1991.

A collection of major statements published in the last hundred years regarding the kind of Greek found in the New Testament; that is, whether it is part of the common language (A. Deissmann, J. H. Moulton, M. Silva), heavily Semitized (C. C. Torrey, M. Black, H. S. Gehman, N. Turner), or somewhere in between (L. Rydbeck, J. A. Fitzmyer). Silva's article is arguably the best single statement regarding the linguistic complexities of studying the Greek of the New Testament.

67 S. Thompson. *The Apocalypse and Semitic Syntax.* SNTSMS 52. Cambridge: Cambridge University Press, 1985.

A volume too much given to explaining every phenomenon of the language of the Apocalypse as some sort of Semitized Greek. This follows his teacher, M. Black (see no. 56).

68 M. Wilcox. *The Semitisms of Acts.* Oxford: Clarendon, 1965.

Follows the pattern set by his teacher, M. Black (see no. 56).

3.3 Syntax and Grammar

Here are placed works that deal with the syntactical structure of the language in all of its complexities. The GRAMCORD computer program is an exceptionally useful tool for syntactical study, since it allows one to search complex strings in a tagged Greek New Testament.

3.3.1 Grammar Books

Although the situation is gradually being remedied, many of the traditional grammars of Greek are now quite old and reflect systems of thought now seen to be outmoded. Much has happened in the last thirty years especially in understanding the complexities of verb structure, cases and prepositions, and discourse features, to name only a few. The reference grammars are indispensable and should not be discounted simply for being old, but they must be treated with caution as well.

69 F. Blass and A. Debrunner. *A Greek Grammar of the New Testament and Other Early Christian Literature.* Translated by R. W. Funk. Chicago: University of Chicago Press, 1961. Original title: *Grammatik des Neutestamentlichen Griechisch.* Göttingen: Vandenhoeck & Ruprecht, 1896. Seventeenth edition revised by F. Rehkopf: 1990.

> The most recent translation of the standard reference grammar of New Testament Greek. It assumes knowledge of classical Greek, not only an unjustified assumption in this day and age but one of dubious linguistic value for learning hellenistic Greek at any time. Explanations are often brief and cryptic, with little helpful exposition. Translations into English of earlier editions were done by H. St. J. Thackeray and J. H. Thayer.

70 J. A. Brooks and C. L. Winbery. *Syntax of New Testament Greek.* Lanham: University Press of America, 1979.

> This teaching grammar serves as a useful replacement for Dana and Mantey (see no. 72), although it unfortunately retains the eight-case system, as well as mixing use of prepositions with simple cases. Reliance upon English is manifest in diagramming as well as understanding of various categories. Subsequent reprintings have seriously improved what once was simply reproduced typescript.

71 E. D. W. Burton. *Syntax of the Moods and Tenses in New Testament Greek.* Chicago: University of Chicago Press, 1893. Third edition: 1900.

A still useful treatment of the moods and tenses of New Testament Greek, consciously fashioned after the treatment of classical Greek by W. W. Goodwin (see no. 73).

72   H. E. Dana and J. R. Mantey. *A Manual Grammar of the Greek New Testament*. New York: Macmillan, 1927.

A grammar based upon the work of A. T. Robertson (see no. 77). Although there are occasional insights, the approach is not consistent, and of course does not reflect thinking later than its own. The cumbersome eight-case system is used, and examples cited are surprisingly few.

73   W. W. Goodwin. *Greek Grammar*. London: Macmillan, 1879.

One of the tried and true classical Greek grammars, although there has been a significant amount of work done since Goodwin's time. Available in many reprints, it is useful for quick consultation. Goodwin also authored the very important *Syntax of the Moods and Tenses of the Greek Verb*. Boston: Ginn/London: Macmillan, 1889 (see no. 71).

74   C. F. D. Moule. *An Idiom Book of New Testament Greek*. Cambridge: Cambridge University Press, 1953. Second edition: 1959.

Moule provides an informative and well-exemplified treatment of the Greek of the New Testament. He toys with some of the modern conceptions of the language. The writing is a bit cryptic at times, making student use occasionally difficult.

75   J. H. Moulton. *Grammar of New Testament Greek*. Edinburgh: T. & T. Clark, 1906–76. I. J. H. Moulton. *Prolegomena*, 1906. Third edition: 1908. II. J. H. Moulton and W. F. Howard. *Accidence and Word-Formation, with an Appendix on Semitisms in the New Testament*, 1929. III. N. Turner. *Syntax*, 1963. IV. N. Turner. *Style*, 1976.

Arguably the most important grammar of New Testament Greek in English. Moulton's two volumes are still brilliant and a mine of information. The reader must know, however, that Moulton's perspective on New Testament Greek as part of hellenistic Greek is not kept by

Turner, who argues for a Semitic form of Greek, almost a Holy Ghost language. Volumes 3 and 4 have rightly been criticized.

76   S. E. Porter. *Idioms of the Greek New Testament.* Biblical Languages: Greek 2. Sheffield: JSOT Press, 1992. Second edition: 1994.

An intermediate grammar that attempts to bring principles of modern linguistics to bear in study of the Greek language. Included are significant chapters on tense and aspect, mood and attitude, conditional clauses, word order and clause structure, and discourse analysis, to name a few.

77   A. T. Robertson. *A Grammar of the Greek New Testament in the Light of Historical Research.* New York: Doran/London: Hodder and Stoughton, 1914. Fourth edition: Nashville: Broadman, 1934.

The longest and most detailed (and sometimes repetitious) grammar of New Testament Greek. Nevertheless, this is a mine of useful information in many areas including morphology as well as syntax.

78   H. W. Smyth. *Greek Grammar.* Cambridge: Harvard University Press, 1920. Revised by G. M. Messing: 1956.

Probably the most thorough and complete description of classical Greek in English, very similar in style and format to W. W. Goodwin (see no. 73). It tends to reflect late nineteenth-century views of the Greek language.

79   G. B. Winer. *A Treatise on the Grammar of New Testament Greek, regarded as a Sure Basis for New Testament Exegesis.* Translated by W. F. Moulton. Edinburgh: T. & T. Clark, 1870. Third edition: 1882. Original title: *Grammatik des Neutestamentlichen Sprachidioms als sicher Grundlage der Neutestamentlichen Exegese.* Leipzig: Vogel, 1822.

The standard translation of a grammar much used and revised in the nineteenth century (also translated by J. H. Thayer). Although Winer follows a very heavily logically based description of the language, there are still many insights and masses of evidence to consider. P. Schmiedel began a revision in 1894 but it was not completed.

80   R. A. Young. *Intermediate New Testament Greek: A Linguistic and Exegetical Approach.* Nashville: Broadman, 1994.

This noteworthy volume adopts Porter's model of Greek verb structure (pp. 105–32; see no. 89) and offers a brief chapter on discourse analysis (pp. 247–66). More questionable is the use of phrase-structure grammar for discussion of the sentence (pp. 205–20).

81   M. Zerwick. *Biblical Greek Illustrated by Examples.* Translated by J. Smith. Rome: Pontifical Biblical Institute, 1963.

Although Zerwick does not treat all subjects and thus does not provide a complete grammar he often has insights that earlier grammarians miss, especially with regard to verb structure.

3.3.2 Monographs and Individual Studies

An often neglected area of research by students because of reliance upon the reference grammars is individual monographs and studies of various dimensions of the Greek language. Verbal aspect has been a subject of great interest lately.

82   B. M. Fanning. *Verbal Aspect in New Testament Greek.* OTM. Oxford: Clarendon, 1990.

The second monograph devoted to this worthwhile topic with reference to the Greek of the New Testament, although far less progressive and insightful than at first sight. The author is still wed to nineteenth-century *Aktionsart* thinking regarding verbs, and fails to distinguish between semantics and pragmatics. Nevertheless, a useful volume.

83   M. J. Harris. "Appendix: Prepositions and Theology in the Greek New Testament." Pp. 1171–1215 in *The New International Dictionary of New Testament Theology.* Vol. 3. Edited by C. Brown. Grand Rapids: Zondervan, 1978.

Theological (but not always linguistic) exposition of the prepositions.

84   M. J. Harris. *Colossians and Philemon.* Exegetical Guide to the Greek New Testament. Grand Rapids: Eerdmans, 1991.

A first attempt to provide exegetical guides to the entire
New Testament. Unfortunately, the use of Greek grammar is already very much out of date, showing very little
if any appreciation of the large amount of work that has
been done in the last thirty years.

85   M. J. Harris. *Jesus as God: The New Testament Use of* Theos
in Reference to Jesus. Grand Rapids: Baker, 1992.

Harris argues that in the New Testament *theos* is used
with reference to Jesus in a number of places, including
John 1:1 and 20:28 as certain, and Rom. 9:5, Titus 2:13,
Heb. 1:8 and 2 Pet. 1:1 as very probable. It is too bad that
he does not consider and use recent work in Greek language and linguistics, and thus bring his discussion up to
date.

86   G. H. R. Horsley (ed.). *New Documents Illustrating Early
Christianity.* Vol. 5. North Ryde, N. S. W., Australia: An-
cient History Documentary Research Centre, Macquarie
University, 1989.

A set of essays by Horsley, dealing with a number of important issues in the study of Greek from the standpoint
of extrabiblical texts such as papyri. Included is a chapter
on the fiction of Jewish Greek (pp. 5–40) and a useful and
revealing critique of N. Turner's *Syntax* (pp. 49–65; see
no. 75).

87   K. L. McKay. *A New Syntax of the Verb in New Testament
Greek: An Aspectual Approach.* SBG 5. New York: Lang,
1993.

Not as new as the title implies, since it is a useful application to New Testament Greek of McKay's theories
worked out in several important journal articles in the
1970s and early 1980s, and not as up to date as Porter and
Fanning (see nos. 89 and 82). It is not strictly speaking a
syntax of the verb either. Of value also is McKay's *Greek
Grammar for Students: A Concise Grammar of Classical
Attic with Special Reference to Aspect in the Verb.* Can-
berra: Australian National University, 1974.

88   B. G. Mandilaras. *Studies in the Greek Language: Some Aspects of the Development of the Greek Language up to the Present Day* (esp. pp. 22–50). Athens: Xenopouls, 1972.

This essay on the relationship between the papyri and the New Testament clarifies many issues regarding their similarities, especially with regard to so-called Semitisms in the New Testament.

89   S. E. Porter. *Verbal Aspect in the Greek of the New Testament, with Reference to Tense and Mood.* SBG 1. New York: Lang, 1989. Second edition: 1993.

The first monograph in English devoted to this topic with reference to the Greek of the New Testament, the author takes bold linguistic steps to show that the Greek verbal system is aspectually and not temporally based. Besides the major tenses and moods, chapters are devoted to conditional clauses, the future tense, and periphrastics.

90   S. E. Porter and D. A. Carson (eds.). *Biblical Greek Language and Linguistics: Open Questions in Current Research.* JSNTSup 72. Sheffield: JSOT Press, 1993.

Part I is devoted to discussion of verb structure. Part II is a collection of essays by various grammarians on such topics as construction grammar by P. Danove, phrase structure by M. Palmer, and discourse analysis of 1 Timothy by J. T. Reed. The volume illustrates continuing strong interest in Greek grammatical study, besides providing excellent individual articles. See also no. 132.

91   F. Stagg. "The Abused Aorist." *JBL* 91 (1972) 222–31.

Stagg's article did for grammar what Barr's book did for lexical study—it cleared the ground and led to rethinking of the meaning of the aorist. See also C. R. Smith. "Errant Aorist Interpreters." *Grace Theological Journal* 2 (1981) 205–26.

92   M. E. Thrall. *Greek Particles in the New Testament: Linguistic and Exegetical Studies.* NTTS 3. Leiden: Brill, 1962.

Often helpful study of particles following the model of similar works by classical scholars such as J. D. Denniston (*The Greek Particles* [Oxford: Clarendon, second edition, 1954]) and J. Blomquist (*Greek Particles in Hellenis-*

tic Prose [Lund: Gleerup, 1969]). The treatment is prelinguistic, and consequently it is difficult to know what exactly counts as evidence and why.

93   N. Turner. *Grammatical Insights into the New Testament.* Edinburgh: T. & T. Clark, 1965.

One of the few books that takes grammatical issues seriously in discussing theological issues, although many of the solutions have not proved convincing.

94   J. W. Voelz. "The Language of the New Testament." Pp. 893–977 in *ANRW* II.25.2. Edited by H. Temporini and W. Haase. Berlin/New York: de Gruyter, 1984.

What amounts to a brief grammar, with a sizable introduction to the nature of the language. Unfortunately, Voelz accepts as consensus that the Greek of the New Testament is Semitic Greek.

3.3.3 Greek Old Testament

95   A. Aejmelaeus. *On the Trail of the Septuagint Translators: Collected Essays.* Kampen: Kok Pharos, 1993.

The volume collects a number of significant essays by Aejmelaeus, including his discussion of the participle and *hoti*, as well as more general treatments of Septuagintal translation technique. Important essays in a neglected area.

96   F. C. Conybeare and St. G. Stock. *A Grammar of Septuagint Greek.* Grand Rapids: Zondervan, 1980. Pp. 25–100 of *Selections from the Septuagint.* Boston: Ginn, 1905.

Still the standard treatment of the grammar of the Septuagint in English, although certainly a very brief treatment. The reprint lacks the reading selections of the original edition.

97   H. St. J. Thackeray. *A Grammar of the Old Testament in Greek according to the Septuagint.* Cambridge: Cambridge University Press, 1909.

The first of several volumes projected but never completed, this one was concerned with questions of introduction, orthography, and accidence, with only a brief treatment of syntax. Nevertheless, it is still very helpful.

3.3.4 Papyri

98 F. T. Gignac. *A Grammar of the Greek Papyri of the Roman and Byzantine Periods.* I. *Phonology.* II. *Morphology.* Milan: Istituto Editoriale Cisalpino-La Giliardica, 1976, 1982.

The standard work on the phonology and morphology of the papyri, with direct relevance to the Greek of the New Testament. The syntax volume(s) is forthcoming.

99 B. Mandilaras. *The Verb in the Greek Non-Literary Papyri.* Athens: Hellenic Ministry of Culture and Sciences, 1973.

The most detailed study of the verb in the papyri, with some appreciation of verbal aspect. Application is occasionally made to the Greek of the New Testament.

100 E. Mayser. *Grammatik der griechischen Papyri aus der Ptolemäerzeit.* 2 vols. Berlin: de Gruyter, 1906–34. Second edition: vol. 1.2 1938, vol. 1.3 1936, vol. 1.1 by H. Schmoll 1970.

Standard grammar of the papyri although superseded in the area of the verb by Mandilaras (see no. 99).

3.4 Lexicography

Lexical study has only recently benefited from modern linguistic method. Most of the standard resources are useful compendia of information although without consistent attention to method and analysis. The Thesaurus Linguae Graecae data base has been heralded as marking a new era in lexical study, since it provides virtually all of the ancient Greek literature in computer accessible format. The data are there, but still require interpretation.

3.4.1 Lexicons

Although there are several smaller lexicons (such as that prepared by R. Bratcher to accompany the *UBSGNT*), many of them are derived from the larger lexicons.

101 G. Abbott-Smith. *A Manual Greek Lexicon of the New Testament.* Edinburgh: T. & T. Clark, 1922. Third edition: 1937.

The publishers do not need to hide the fact that this is an older work (as they apparently do in the reprint of 1986), since it stands on its own merits. The advantage is frequent reference to the Septuagint and Hebrew words where appropriate. There is also a useful appendix of irregular verbs.

102 W. Bauer. *A Greek-English Lexicon of the New Testament and Other Early Christian Literature.* Translated and revised by W. F. Arndt and F. W. Gingrich. Chicago/London: University of Chicago Press, 1957. Original title: *Griechisch-Deutsches Wörterbuch zu den Schriften des Neuen Testaments und der übrigen urchristlichen Literatur.* Berlin: de Gruyter, fourth edition, 1949–52. Fifth edition: 1957–58. Revised by F. W. Gingrich and F. W. Danker: 1979.

The standard New Testament Greek lexicon, although to be used with caution, since it is not always linguistic in its judgments nor consistent in its organization. The sixth German edition by K. and B. Aland came out in 1988. See also J. R. Alsop (ed.). *An Index to the Revised Bauer-Arndt-Gingrich Greek Lexicon Second Edition by F. W. Gingrich and F. W. Danker.* Grand Rapids: Zondervan, 1981.

103 G. W. H. Lampe. *A Patristic Greek Lexicon.* Oxford: Clarendon, 1961.

Useful but limited because of the sheer bulk of patristic writing.

104 H. G. Liddell and R. Scott, revised by H. S. Jones with R. McKenzie. *A Greek-English Lexicon.* Oxford: Clarendon, 1843. Ninth edition: 1940. Supplement: 1968.

Still perhaps the best lexicon of an ancient language ever done. A necessary tool.

105 J. P. Louw and E. A. Nida (eds.). *Greek-English Lexicon of the New Testament based on Semantic Domains.* 2 vols. New York: United Bible Societies, 1988.

Much criticized (much of it unjustly) but highly useful and ambitious lexicon of the New Testament that gives more than lip-service to the principles of modern linguistics, in particular the concept of semantic fields. Vocabulary of the New Testament is arranged not alphabetically but by domain, so that polysemous words appear several times (as is appropriate). See Nida and Louw's monograph for further support (no. 122).

106 J. H. Moulton and G. Milligan. *The Vocabulary of the Greek Testament Illustrated from the Papyri and Other Non-Literary Sources.* London: Hodder and Stoughton, 1914–29. Reprinted Grand Rapids: Eerdmans, 1980.

A still invaluable source of information regarding how the Greek found in the New Testament is paralleled with usage in nonliterary texts—the first tool of its kind in English to transmit this valuable information to a wider reading public.

107 J. H. Thayer. *A Greek-English Lexicon of the New Testament being Grimm's Wilke's Clavis Novi Testamenti.* New York/Cincinnati/Chicago: American Book Company, 1886. Corrected edition: 1889.

Outmoded in many respects, especially since it was written before the evidence from the papyri was known.

3.4.2 Concordances to the Greek Bible

108 K. Aland with H. Bachmann and W. Slaby (eds.). *Vollständige Konkordanz zum Griechischen Neuen Testament: Unter Zugrundelegung aller kritischen Textausgaben und des Textus Receptus.* 2 vols. Berlin/New York: de Gruyter, 1975–78.

The standard concordance, but prohibitively expensive. Includes many word statistics.

109 H. Bachmann and W. Slaby. *A Computer Concordance to the Novum Testamentum Graece.* Berlin/New York: de Gruyter, 1985.

A more affordable modern concordance.

110 E. Hatch and H. E. Redpath. *A Concordance to the Septuagint and Other Greek Versions of the Old Testament.* 3 vols. Oxford: Clarendon, 1897–1906. Reprinted Grand Rapids: Baker, 1987.

Still useful as a concordance to the Septuagint.

111 W. F. Moulton and A. S. Geden. *A Concordance to the Greek Testament.* Edinburgh: T. & T. Clark, 1897. Fifth edition revised by H. K. Moulton: 1978.

Still the easiest and handiest printed concordance to use (besides the most reasonable to purchase), although based upon earlier editions of the Greek New Testament, in particular Westcott and Hort's.

112 A. Schmoller. *Handkonkordanz zum Griechischen Neuen Testament*. Stuttgart: Wurttembergische Bibelanstalt, 1938.

Not complete but very handy to use.

113 W. C. Trenchard. *The Student's Complete Vocabulary Guide to the Greek New Testament.* Grand Rapids: Zondervan, 1992.

This vocabulary guide pretty much makes the other ones by B. Metzger, T. Robinson and others obsolete, although it is perhaps not as handy and portable as some of the others.

3.4.3 Theological Dictionaries and Vocabulary Studies

There has been much bad work done in this area, primarily because interpreters have wanted to ground their theologies in individual vocabulary items, apparently believing that this would substantiate these concepts in a more concrete way. The confusion of word and concept is rampant in many of these tools, as is overtheologizing a given context on the basis of presence of a lexical item. This is not to say that many of these tools do not also have valuable information. One must be cautious.

114 H. Balz and G. Schneider (eds.). *Exegetical Dictionary of the New Testament*. 3 vols. Grand Rapids: Eerdmans/Edinburgh: T. & T. Clark, 1990–93. Original title: *Exegetisches Wörterbuch zum Neuen Testament*. 3 vols. Stuttgart: Kohlhammer, 1980–83. Second edition: 1992.

A smaller Kittel well researched and useful.

115 C. Brown (ed.). *The New International Dictionary of New Testament Theology*. 4 vols. Grand Rapids: Zondervan/ Exeter: Paternoster, 1975–79, with Scripture Index by D. Townsley and R. Bjork, 1985. Translation and revision of L. Coenen, E. Beyreuther and H. Bietenhard (eds.). *Theologisches Begriffslexikon zum Neuen Testament*. Wuppertal: Brockhaus, 1967–71.

Promoted as an update on Kittel, although the articles added by Brown and his team are better. The major step forward is that the organization is by English subject and so not restricted to a single Greek word.

116 D. Hill. *Greek Words and Hebrew Meanings: Studies in the Semantics of Soteriological Terms.* SNTSMS 5. Cambridge: Cambridge University Press, 1967.

One of the first studies in the light of Barr's strictures regarding semantics. His conclusions are still valuable, although probably weighted a bit too much toward the Semitic side.

117 G. Kittel and G. Friedrich (eds.). *Theological Dictionary of the New Testament.* Translated by G. W. Bromiley. 10 vols. Grand Rapids: Eerdmans, 1964–76. Original title: *Theologisches Wörterbuch zum Neuen Testament.* Stuttgart: Kohlhammer, 1933–73.

A valuable and useful tool with all of its masses of information but also with all of its many flaws: theological lexicography, confusion of word and concept, emphasis of diachronic over synchronic history and indefensible dichotomies regarding the supposed Hebrew and Greek mindsets.

118 N. Turner. *Christian Words.* Edinburgh: T. & T. Clark, 1980.

Theological lexicography at its most unconvincing. The concept of a Christian word is one that needs much further examination.

3.4.4 Monographs and Individual Studies

119 A. Deissmann. *Bible Studies.* Translated by A. Grieve. Edinburgh: T. & T. Clark, 1901. Second edition: 1903. Original titles: *Bibelstudien.* Marburg: Elwert, 1895, and *Neue Bibelstudien.* Marburg: Elwert, 1897.

Excellent essays on various dimensions of the New Testament in relation to the then recently discovered papyri, especially in terms of lexicography. Deissmann's famous and probably not defensible distinction between letters and epistles is found here (pp. 3–59).

120 C. J. Hemer. "Reflections on the Nature of New Testament Greek Vocabulary." *TynBul* 38 (1987) 65–92.

Important recent summary statement regarding the character of Greek vocabulary, discussing its place within the hellenistic world and in relation to possible Semitic influence. Hemer's knowledge of the nonliterary sources is evident.

121 J. P. Louw (ed.). *Lexicography and Translation, with Special Reference to Bible Translation.* Roggebaai, Cape Town: Bible Society of South Africa, 1985.

Especially important are three essays by Louw himself on dictionaries (pp. 53–81), the present state of New Testament lexicography (pp. 97–117), and a semantic domain approach to lexicography (pp. 157–97).

122 E. A. Nida and J. P. Louw. *Lexical Semantics of the Greek New Testament.* SBLRBS 25. Atlanta: Scholars Press, 1992.

This volume provides further theoretical and exemplary justification for the construction of the UBS lexicon (see no. 105), brought on no doubt in response to criticism (much of it unfounded) of the lexicon.

123 M. Silva. *Biblical Words and their Meaning: An Introduction to Lexical Semantics.* Grand Rapids: Zondervan, 1983. Revised edition: 1994.

The first book of its kind for New Testament study, it is not highly original but it does translate into terms meaningful terminology employed in lexical semantics for New Testament scholars. The first part is concerned with historical linguistics, perhaps relevant for New Testament studies in the light of the Septuagint, and the second with what he calls descriptive semantics. Silva is heavily dependent upon S. Ullmann and J. Lyons, not bad choices among linguists.

124 A. C. Thiselton. "Semantics and New Testament Interpretation." Pp. 75–104 in *New Testament Interpretation: Essays on Principles and Methods.* Edited by I. H. Marshall. Grand Rapids: Eerdmans/Exeter: Paternoster, 1977.

Perhaps the best overview of the subject written for New Testament students.

3.5 Style and Discourse Analysis

Stylistics or the study of an author's style has been a part of looking at the language of the New Testament for centuries. It is only recently that more quantifiable criteria have been applied to the area. Related to stylistics is discourse analysis. Discourse analysis is an area of high activity in application of linguistic methodology to the biblical text. It is not so well known, however, that there are several schools of thought on discourse analysis. In the United States, the method is dominated by the Summer Institute of Linguistics. See also Porter (no. 76) and Cotterell and Turner (no. 51), who have sections on discourse analysis.

125 D. A. Black with K. Barnwell and S. Levinsohn (eds.). *Linguistics and New Testament Interpretation: Essays on Discourse Analysis*. Nashville: Broadman, 1992.

> One of the first collections of papers on discourse analysis designed for New Testament students. The SIL approach is exemplified. Contributors of note are J. P. Louw, S. Levinsohn, J. C. Callow, K. Callow, H. Van Dyke Parunak, and R. Longacre.

126 K. Callow. *Discourse Considerations in Translating the Word of God.* Grand Rapids: Zondervan, 1974.

> A fine survey of discourse factors to consider when translating.

127 A. Kenny. *A Stylometric Study of the New Testament.* Oxford: Clarendon, 1986.

> A large number of stylometric tests are made of the Greek New Testament. In the Pauline corpus only Titus appears to be under suspicion regarding authorship on the basis of style.

128 S. H. Levinsohn. *Discourse Features of New Testament Greek: A Coursebook*. Dallas: Summer Institute of Linguistics, 1992.

> A helpful introduction to the kind of discourse analysis practiced by SIL. This is certainly not the only (or even most useful) kind of discourse analysis, but merits exploration by students of the New Testament.

129 J. P. Louw. "Discourse Analysis and the Greek New Testament." *Bible Translator* 24 (1973) 101–18.

One of the first essays in the field. Louw's colon analysis has not been to everyone's liking.

130 E. A. Nida, J. P. Louw, A. H. Snyman, and J. V. W. Cronje. *Style and Discourse: With Special Relevance to the Text of the Greek New Testament*. Roggebaai, Cape Town: Bible Society, 1983.

An introductory treatment of discourse analysis with attention to matters of rhetoric, displaying the South African orientation.

131 S. E. Porter and J. T. Reed. "Greek Grammar since BDF: A Retrospective and Prospective Analysis." *FN* 4 (1991) 143–64.

An assessment of Blass and Debrunner's grammar (see no. 69) is followed by discussion of the importance of verbal aspect theory and discourse analysis, proposing these as important areas for future work.

132 S. E. Porter and D. A. Carson (eds.). *Discourse Analysis and Other Topics in Biblical Greek* . JSNTSup 113. Sheffield: Sheffield Academic Press, 1995.

Part One is devoted to discussion of discourse analysis, with an introductory survey by S. E. Porter and application to Philippians by J. T. Reed, G. H. Guthrie, and S. Levinsohn (see no. 128), with responses by M. Silva and S. E. Porter. M. Palmer has an essay using discourse analysis to discuss Rom. 4:1 in Part Two.

133 A. B. Spencer. *Paul's Literary Style: A Stylistic and Historical Comparison of II Corinthians 11:16–12:13, Romans 8:9–39, and Philippians 3:2–4:13*. ETS Monograph. Jackson, MS: Evangelical Theological Society, 1984.

To be commended for being one of the first attempts to analyze style in New Testament writers, but one flawed by faulty method and too small a sample.

3.6 Translation Theory

Translation theory is not something that linguists pay much attention to. And neither is the ability to translate into another language a sign of one's linguistic competence. But for Bible students translation theory is of importance. There has been much debate recently regarding what translation is. How much interpretation is there in translation? Is it possible or even desirable to eliminate interpretation in translation? What does it mean to do a literal translation? What does it mean to do a dynamic translation? Which one is to be preferred, when, and for what purpose? What role does paraphrase play in translation? These are just some of the questions asked regarding translation. There is no simple answer, and there is no single way of translating.

134 J. Beekman and J. Callow. *Translating the Word of God.* Grand Rapids: Zondervan, 1974.

> A very useful guide to the complexities of Bible translation. This volume helps to show that translation requires much more than a lexicon.

135 E. A. Nida. *Toward a Science of Translating with Special Reference to Principles and Procedures Involved in Bible Translating.* Leiden: Brill, 1964.

> A classic treatment of the issue of translation. The discussion of the history of translation alone is almost worth the price of the book.

136 E. A. Nida and C. R. Taber. *The Theory and Practice of Translation.* Helps for Translators. Leiden: Brill, 1969.

> The Bible for Bible Society translation, with its development of the idea of kernel sentences and transfer from source to receptor languages.

137 H. M. Orlinsky and R. G. Bratcher. *A History of Bible Translation and the North American Contribution.* Atlanta: Scholars Press, 1991.

> In many ways a tribute to the work of the late Orlinsky. This volume is both a description of the four major periods in the history of Bible translation and an evaluation and assessment of various translations. Certain ones come off better than others, with the ones that Orlinsky and Bratcher have been involved in usually looking best.

138 J. H. Skilton (ed.). *The New Testament Student and Bible Translation.* The New Testament Student 4. Phillipsburg, N.J.: Presbyterian and Reformed, 1978.

Some of the few defenses of the so-called formal equivalence translation theory are found here. To some extent
this illustrates how difficult it is to defend this approach.

139 J. De Waard and E. A. Nida. *From One Language to Another:
Functional Equivalence in Bible Translating.* Nashville:
Nelson, 1986.

Discusses theories of translation from the perspective of
"functional equivalence" (which used to be dynamic
equivalence, apparently until it raised too many hackles).

3.7 Epistolary Form

The letter form, the genre of the Gospels and the genre of Acts
are arguably the most important literary questions regarding the
New Testament. Serious discussion of the form of the letter
began with A. Deissmann (see nos. 119, 475), who made the distinction between epistle and letter proper. Most do not hold to
this distinction any more. Study of the ancient Greek letter has
been carried on for the most part by New Testament scholars, not
only because the form is so important for the New Testament itself but because classical scholars have not given it much attention. Within the last twenty years interest in the letter has increased dramatically, with detailed studies of various parts of the
letter. There is much primary literature available in the form of
ancient Greek letters both nonliterary and literary (e.g., Plato's
letters). In some ways the letters of the New Testament are
unique since they have many characteristics of both categories of
letters. Recent discussion has focused upon the major parts of the
letters (thanksgiving, body, closing), including how they are recognized, their significant features, and what they convey (most of
the claims for what they convey are overdone).

3.7.1 Primary Texts

There are a number of collections of papyri letters that give a
good idea of how the New Testament letters compare. Other papyrus collections will also need to be consulted.

140 W. H. Davis. *Greek Papyri of the First Century.* New York/
London: Harper and Brothers, 1933. Reprinted Chicago:
Ares, 1960.

141   A. S. Hunt and C. C. Edgar. *Select Papyri.* I. *Non-Literary Papyri Private Affairs.* LCL. Cambridge: Harvard University Press/London: Heinemann. II. *Non-Literary Papyri Public Documents.* LCL. Cambridge: Harvard University Press/London: Heinemann.

   Still a standard collection by two of the most important scholars of the papyri letters. There is a third volume of literary papyri.

142   A. J. Malherbe (ed.). *Ancient Epistolary Theorists.* SBLSBS 19. Atlanta: Scholars Press, 1988.

   The major texts of those who theorized about letter writing in the ancient world, in Greek and Latin with translations and helpful introduction.

143   H. G. Meecham. *Light from Ancient Letters.* London: George Allen & Unwin, 1923.

   A useful collection of papyri letters, with translations and notes.

144   G. Milligan. *Selections from the Greek Papyri.* Cambridge: Cambridge University Press, 1910.

   A useful collection of papyri letters, with translations and notes, by one of the first to realize the importance of the papyri for study of the New Testament.

145   J. L. White. *Light from Ancient Letters.* FF. Philadelphia: Fortress, 1986.

   An excellent collection of illustrative papyrus letters, with translation and exposition, as well as an informative essay on letters in the ancient Greco-Roman world. White has done more than anyone else in the study of the letter in relation to the New Testament.

3.7.2 Analysis of Letters

146   W. G. Doty. "The Classification of Epistolary Literature." *CBQ* 31 (1969) 183–99.

   An important attempt to quantify and classify epistolary forms.

147   W. G. Doty. *Letters in Primitive Christianity.* GBS. Philadelphia: Fortress, 1973.

A generally reliable, short guide to the letter form in primitive Christianity, especially Paul's letters, although there are a few claims made for the letter form that probably go beyond what can be asserted in relation to ancient epistolary practice.

148 R. W. Funk. "The Apostolic Parousia: Form and Significance." Pp. 249–68 in *Christian History and Interpretation: Studies Presented to J. Knox*. Edited by W. R. Farmer, C. F. D. Moule and R. R. Niebuhr. Cambridge: Cambridge University Press, 1967.

Funk's important study of Paul's references to his intended visits, in the light of their function to establish and maintain his apostolic authority. See also no. 43.

149 P. T. O'Brien. *Introductory Thanksgivings in the Letters of Paul*. NovTSup 49. Leiden: Brill, 1977.

Standard treatment of the introductory thanksgiving, but one that probably gives too much importance to it so far as forecasting the agenda of the letter.

150 E. R. Richards. *The Secretary in the Letters of Paul*. WUNT 2.42. Tübingen: Mohr-Siebeck, 1991.

Not always convincing or accurate use of ancient sources, but provocative book that raises important questions regarding transmission process.

151 F. Schnider and W. Stenger. *Studien zum neutestamentlichen Briefformular*. NTTS 11. Leiden: Brill, 1987.

A detailed study of the epistolary opening and closing in terms primarily of the New Testament, with emphasis upon the various formulas that indicate the letter divisions.

152 M. L. Stirewalt, Jr. *Studies in Ancient Greek Epistolography*. SBLRBS 27. Atlanta: Scholars Press, 1993.

At long last the promised published essays. Are they worth it? Perhaps. Stirewalt goes over much old ground, but does show that Deissmann's distinction between letter and epistle is one that the ancients did not make.

153 S. K. Stowers. *Letter Writing in Greco-Roman Antiquity*. LEC 5. Philadelphia: Westminster, 1986.

A useful collection of letters in translation, although Stowers is not always convincing in his categorizations.

154 J. L. White. *The Form and Function of the Body of the Greek Letter: A Study of the Letter-Body in the Non-Literary Papyri and in Paul the Apostle.* SBLDS 2. Missoula: Scholars Press, 1972.

The most detailed study of the body of the Greek letter. Debate continues regarding the divisions and distinguishing features of the body.

155 J. L. White (ed.). *Studies in Ancient Letter Writing. Semeia* 22. Chico: Scholars Press, 1981.

Essays by J. L. White and C. H. Kim on the Greek letter and J. A. Fitzmyer on the Aramaic letter, among others.

156 J. L. White. "New Testament Epistolary Literature in the Framework of Ancient Epistolography." Pp. 1730–56 in *ANRW* II.25.2. Edited by H. Temporini and W. Haase. Berlin/New York: de Gruyter, 1984.

An excellent summary of the relation of New Testament letters to ancient epistolography by the person who has probably studied the issue more than anyone else.

Part 2

New Testament Criticism and History of Interpretation

4

The Text and Textual Criticism

Textual criticism is a more complex discipline than might at first appear, and it is certainly more complex than is often conveyed in exegesis courses. Textual criticism demands far more than a critical apparatus to be done well. Although textual criticism was actually formalized as a discipline by the Alexandrian librarians during the hellenistic period, modern textual criticism is only about two hundred years old. There are currently a number of issues that are continually debated. For example, are internal or external criteria more important, how are manuscripts classified and analyzed, which manuscripts are given priority? While it is fair to say that the so-called neutral text of Westcott and Hort is no longer given privileged status, the Alexandrian text is still given priority in most of the eclectic texts, despite the continued debate of those who wish to give priority to internal factors alone or to non-Alexandrian texts.

4.1 Greek Texts of the Bible

4.1.1 New Testament

157 K. Aland, M. Black, C. M. Martini, B. M. Metzger, and A. Wikgren (eds.). *The Greek New Testament.* New York/ London/Edinburgh/Amsterdam/Stuttgart: United Bible Societies, 1966. Second edition: 1968. Third edition: 1975. Third corrected edition: 1983.

The standard edition of the Greek New Testament, although revised in what some would consider an inferior fourth edition (see no. 158). This edition is characterized by a very readable font, with an apparatus that has approximately 1400 entries giving extensive attestation to witnesses.

158 B. Aland, K. Aland, J. Karavidopulos, C. M. Martini, and B. M. Metzger (eds.). *The Greek New Testament.* Stuttgart: Deutsche Bibelgesellschaft, fourth edition, 1993.

Although the text is the same as that of the third edition and hence is the same as the Nestle and Aland text, this fourth edition is bound to raise serious questions, since there appears to be a move toward making this the new established text. Noticeable is the "inflation" of ratings of readings.

159 Z. C. Hodges and A. L. Farstad (eds.). *The Greek New Testament according to the Majority Text.* Nashville: Nelson, 1982.

Hard to believe that some still argue for this text as the most reliable, but they do. Here is the latest edition of it, which has met with mixed reviews.

160 G. D. Kilpatrick (ed.). *H KAINH ΔIAΘHKH.* London: British and Foreign Bible Society, second edition, 1958.

An edition with minimal critical apparatus.

161 E. Nestle and K. Aland (eds.). *Novum Testamentum Graece.* Stuttgart: Deutsche Bibelgesellschaft, twenty-sixth edition, 1979 (first edition 1898) and twenty-seventh edition, 1993.

The same text as the *UBSGNT*, but with a larger number of variants treated in not as much detail. The critical apparatus is by K. and B. Aland. The latest edition includes several major revisions including a fresh review of Greek and Latin patristic citations and an expanded list of manuscripts. A helpful revision.

162 A. Souter (ed.). *Novum Testamentum Graece.* Oxford: Clarendon, 1910. Second edition: 1947.

Edition in the Oxford Classical Texts series, by the well-known classical scholar and textual critic.

163 C. Tischendorf (ed.). *Novum Testamentum Graece.* 2 vols. Leipzig: Giesecke & Devrient, eighth edition, 1869, 1872.

> One of the most important critical texts done. Still to be consulted.

4.1.2 Greek Old Testament

164 Academia Litterarum Gottingensis. *Septuaginta: Vetus Testamentum Graecum.* Göttingen: Vandenhoeck & Ruprecht, 1931–.

> Still in process, the Göttingen Septuagint promises to be the best critical edition, although certainly not the most portable with one volume per biblical book usually.

165 A. Rahlfs (ed.). *Septuaginta.* Stuttgart: Deutsche Bibelgesellschaft, 1935. Reprinted: 1979.

> Available in one or two volume printings, this is the standard complete text of the Septuagint.

166 H. B. Swete (ed.). *The Old Testament in Greek according to the Septuagint.* Cambridge: Cambridge University Press, 1887–94. Third edition: 1901–7 (vol. 1, fourth edition, 1909).

> Still a useful edition, especially in canonical discussions, but also elsewhere.

167 A. E. Brooke, N. McLean, and H. St. J. Thackeray (eds.). *The Old Testament in Greek according to the Text of Codex Vaticanus.* 3 vols. Cambridge: Cambridge University Press, 1906–40.

> An edition based upon Vaticanus. This text is not widely used in our eclectic age.

4.2 Textual Criticism

4.2.1 Introductions and Handbooks

The following list of books includes basic introductions to textual criticism and a number of the standard handbooks. The handbooks usually include the same basic information—although often not nearly so well presented as in the introductions—along with more detailed discussions of the individual manuscripts.

168 K. Aland and B. Aland. *The Text of the New Testament: An Introduction to the Critical Editions and to the Theory and Practice of Modern Textual Criticism.* Translated by E. F. Rhodes. Grand Rapids: Eerdmans/Leiden: Brill, 1987. Second edition: 1989. Original title: *Der Text des Neuen Testaments: Einführung in die wissenschaftlichen Ausgaben so wie in Theorie und Praxis der modernen Textkritik.* Stuttgart: Deutsche Bibelgesellschaft, 1982.

A very helpful introduction to textual criticism by two of the current leaders. Advocates of the Alexandrian textual tradition.

169 J. N. Birdsall. "The Recent History of New Testament Textual Criticism (from Westcott and Hort, 1881, to the Present)." Pp. 99–197 in *ANRW* II.26.1. Edited by W. Haase. Berlin/New York: de Gruyter, 1992.

An excellent survey of the development of the discipline, with discussion of the various methods currently being practiced, as well as a useful survey of the major manuscripts and versions and the editions in which they are available.

170 F. F. Bruce. *The New Testament Documents: Are They Reliable?* Downers Grove: InterVarsity, 1943. Original title: *Are the New Testament Documents Reliable?* Fifth edition: 1960.

A very useful volume to introduce the student to the major questions regarding the development and historical reliability of the New Testament documents, first written from Bruce's then position as classicist.

171 P. W. Comfort. *The Quest for the Original Text of the New Testament.* Grand Rapids: Baker, 1992.

Argues against the *UBSGNT* and for noneclectic texts following particular manuscripts, especially the papyri. He is confident of finding the original text. His work has been strongly criticized for being full of errors.

172 D. Ewert. *From Ancient Tablets to Modern Translations: A General Introduction to the Bible.* Grand Rapids: Zondervan, 1983.

A history of the history of the Bible, from earliest written forms to modern translations. Generally a fine overview, but frequently confuses history and theology and offers uncritically traditional conclusions.

173 J. H. Greenlee. *Introduction to New Testament Textual Criticism*. Grand Rapids: Eerdmans, 1964. Revised edition: Peabody: Hendrickson, 1995.

A beginning text in the Westcott and Hort tradition. Greenlee does not assume that the student knows much. He includes two chapters on praxis. An even more basic treatment is J. H. Greenlee. *Scribes, Scrolls, and Scripture: A Student's Guide to New Testament Textual Criticism*. Grand Rapids: Eerdmans, 1985.

174 F. G. Kenyon. *The Text of the Greek Bible*. London: Duckworth, 1936. Third edition revised by A. W. Adams: 1975.

A study in the Westcott and Hort mode of the varieties of texts available for studying the Greek Bible, updated by Adams and still of use.

175 B. M. Metzger. *The Text of the New Testament: Its Transmission, Corruption and Restoration*. Oxford: Clarendon, 1964. Third edition: 1992.

The third edition is the second edition with a new extended preface. Nevertheless, this work remains the standard work on textual criticism of the New Testament and is very useful as a text and reference book.

176 E. Nestle. *Introduction to the Textual Criticism of the New Testament*. Translated by W. Edie and A. Menzies. London: Williams and Norgate, 1901.

Written before some of the more recent finds and many of the current debates, but a thorough treatment by one of the important editors of the Greek New Testament.

177 G. Milligan. *The New Testament and its Transmission*. London: Hodder and Stoughton, 1932.

An introduction to the text of the New Testament that is truly introductory, discussing how manuscripts were originally written, the nature and kinds of manuscripts and versions, the critical editions and early English versions.

178 A. Souter. *The Text and Canon of the New Testament.* London: Duckworth, 1912. Revised edition by C. S. C. Williams: 1954.

A useful introduction to textual criticism in the Westcott and Hort tradition. Still a valuable resource for canon research.

179 S. P. Tregelles. *An Account of the Printed Text of the Greek New Testament, with Remarks on its Revision upon Critical Principles.* London: Bagster, 1854.

Tregelles's classic discussion, still helpful, includes a collation of the major editions of the Greek New Testament to that time.

180 L. Vaganay. *An Introduction to New Testament Textual Criticism.* Translated by J. Heimerdinger. Cambridge: Cambridge University Press, 1991. Original French edition: L. Vaganay, *Initiation à la critique textuelle du Nouveau Testament.* Paris: Cerf, 1934. Translation of revised and expanded second edition by C.-B. Amphoux: 1986.

A significant study of textual criticism, especially the nature and types of the texts available, with emphasis upon the earliness of the Western text and discussion of the versions.

181 B. F. Westcott and F. J. A. Hort. *The New Testament in the Original Greek.* 2 vols. Cambridge: Macmillan, 1881/New York: Harper and Brothers, 1882. Second edition: 1896, 1898.

The classic treatment that though now widely disputed still sets the standard for textual criticism, no matter what others may claim. Westcott and Hort emphasized their so-called neutral text, which was an early form of the Alexandrian text. Despite much discussion the Alexandrian text still forms the basis of modern eclectic critical texts.

4.2.2 Praxis

In many ways these books are similar to those in 2.1 above, except that they place a greater emphasis upon actually doing textual criticism, often in the form of exercises, but also in terms of more extensive discussions of actual problems.

182 J. Finegan. *Encountering New Testament Manuscripts: A Working Introduction to Textual Criticism.* Grand Rapids: Eerdmans, 1974/London: SPCK, 1975.

> One of the best tools for learning textual criticism, because plenty of pictures of texts are included to give a sense of what is being dealt with.

183 B. M. Metzger (ed.). *A Textual Commentary on the Greek New Testament: A Companion Volume to the United Bible Societies' Greek New Testament.* London/New York: United Bible Societies, 1971 (on *UBSGNT*[3]). Corrected edition: 1975. Second edition: 1994 (on *UBSGNT*[4]).

> An invaluable tool when working with the Greek text of the New Testament, since it gives an idea of how the editorial committee decided on the variants selected.

184 R. Renehan. *Greek Textual Criticism: A Reader.* Cambridge: Harvard University Press, 1969.

> An introduction to the textual criticism of classical texts, but with application to the New Testament, which is cited occasionally. This is a valuable book in that it demonstrates a textual critic at work.

4.2.3 Detailed Studies

In the light of the various methodologies employed in textual criticism, here are several detailed studies of issues, including a number of volumes that collect together papers by well-known practitioners of textual criticism. Section 2.1 should also be consulted, since several of the handbooks reflect the distinctive perspectives of their authors.

185 D. A. Carson. *The King James Debate: A Plea for Realism.* Grand Rapids: Baker, 1979.

> An argument against the exaltation of the King James version. Must reading especially for those who opt for the AV.

186 B. D. Ehrman. *The Orthodox Corruption of Scripture: The Effect of Early Christological Controversies on the Text of the New Testament.* New York/Oxford: Oxford University Press, 1993.

> Ehrman attempts to integrate textual criticism into the mainstream of New Testament studies by showing how

Christological beliefs influenced scribal habits and behavior. Thus theological questions need to be considered more fully in doing textual criticism. Perhaps he gets carried away but still offers an important note of caution.

187 E. C. Colwell. *Studies in Methodology in Textual Criticism of the New Testament*. NTTS 9. Leiden: Brill, 1969.

A collection of Colwell's essays, instrumental in establishing the Claremont method of genealogical relationships among manuscripts. Included also is his essay attempting to revive Westcott and Hort against unnecessary criticism.

188 J. K. Elliott. *Essays and Studies in New Testament Textual Criticism*. Estudios de Filología Neotestamentaria 3. Córdoba: Ediciones El Almendro, 1992.

A collection of essays by this thoroughgoing eclectic critic, following in the footsteps of his mentor, G. D. Kilpatrick (see no. 191). Some are broad essays and others are very specific.

189 E. J. Epp and G. D. Fee. *Studies in the Theory and Method of New Testament Textual Criticism*. SD 45. Grand Rapids: Eerdmans, 1993.

A collection of these well-known textual critics' significant essays. Although they generally share the same perspective (and consequently there is some overlap), they clearly define their position in relation to other methods of textual criticism, including that of the Alands and G. D. Kilpatrick.

190 H. Y. Gamble, Jr. *The Textual History of the Letter to the Romans: A Study in Textual and Literary Criticism*. SD 42. Grand Rapids: Eerdmans, 1977.

Not only the definitive study to date on this intriguing textual problem (or these problems) but a model of how to do textual criticism, weighing the internal and external evidence judiciously. His conclusions have merit with regard to the integrity of the letter (ch. 16 was part of the original letter) and the later addition of the doxology (16.25–27). His discussion of epistolary closings is excellent.

191 G. D. Kilpatrick. *The Principles and Practice of New Testament Textual Criticism: Collected Essays of G. D. Kilpatrick.* Edited by J. K. Elliott. BETL 96. Leuven: Leuven University Press/Peeters, 1990.

Many of the most important papers illustrating the thoroughgoing eclectic methodology of Kilpatrick are gathered here by his disciple, J. K. Elliott.

192 B. M. Metzger. *The Early Versions of the New Testament: Their Origin, Transmission and Limitations.* Oxford: Clarendon, 1977.

All of the versions up to A.D. 1000 are discussed. Recent textual criticism often sees great value in examining the versions.

193 H. A. Sturz. *The Byzantine Text-Type and New Testament Textual Criticism.* Nashville: Nelson, 1984.

A valiant though limited attempt to justify the Byzantine text-type. Although plausible arguments are created, they are not as convincing as they need to be to be persuasive.

194 G. Zuntz. *The Text of the Epistles: A Disquisition upon the Corpus Paulinum.* Schweich Lectures 1946. London: British Academy, 1953.

Textual criticism by a classical scholar of repute in the area of textual criticism of Euripides. He explores the characteristics of p46, the earliest Pauline papyrus text.

4.2.4 Introductions to the Greek Old Testament

195 S. Jellicoe. *The Septuagint and Modern Study.* Oxford: Clarendon, 1968.

A standard treatment of the Septuagint, by one of the recent masters of the text.

196 H. B. Swete. *An Introduction to the Old Testament in Greek, with an Appendix Containing the Letter of Aristeas.* Edited by H. St. J. Thackeray. Cambridge: Cambridge University Press, 1900. Second edition: 1902.

In some ways still the best introduction to the Septuagint.

5

Literary Criticism

Literary criticism is the most diverse of all of the criticisms, since it is not entirely clear what is meant by literary criticism of the New Testament. In many respects redaction criticism is a form of literary criticism in its appreciation of the theological (or ideational) interests of the Gospel writers. For most literary critics, however, literary criticism means something else. But what is this? For some it is a reading of the final form of the text as if it were a free-standing artifact (New Criticism or a type of formalism). This is still a major form of literary criticism of the New Testament. For others it is a reading of the text to determine the intention of the original author (biographical criticism). For others it is an attempt to reconstruct the response of the original first-century readers (dubiously called reader-response criticism, but the predominant form). For others it is an attempt to discover and exploit the internal contradictions of the text (deconstruction). Formalist or new-critical readings arrived on the scene first and have been the most prevalent, although they have been open to the criticism of naiveté as they "discover" what many consider to be self-evident conclusions. More recently, there has been far more of what has been termed reader-response criticism or deconstruction. Some of this is quite clever, although if one still holds to the (perhaps outmoded in some people's eyes) view that interpretation is about finding out more about the text and not the interpreter, then much of this may not be particularly useful. Many treatments of the parables have taken what may be called literary approaches.

197 R. Alter and F. Kermode (eds.). *The Literary Guide to the Bible*. Cambridge: Harvard University Press/London: Collins, 1987.

> The New Testament essays are not generally as convincing as the Old Testament ones, but that may be because literary analysis of the New Testament is less well developed.

198 J. C. Anderson and S. D. Moore (eds.). *Mark and Method: New Approaches in Biblical Studies*. Minneapolis: Fortress, 1992.

> Five kinds of criticism—narrative, reader-response, deconstruction, feminist and sociological—are exemplified, in other words four literary criticisms.

199 D. E. Aune. *The New Testament in its Literary Environment*. LEC 8. Philadelphia: Westminster, 1987/Cambridge: J. Clarke, 1988.

> A generic approach to the literature of the New Testament, placing it within its ancient literary context. Among other things, Aune gives credibility to the idea that Luke–Acts may fit within the genre of historical writing and analyses of ancient epistolary form.

200 J. L. Bailey and L. D. Vander Broek. *Literary Forms in the New Testament*. Louisville: Westminster/John Knox/London: SPCK, 1992.

> A brief but useful guide to the various literary forms and types found in the New Testament. Almost all of the categories beg for fuller exposition, and a number of types at different levels are all treated similarly. But this will point the exegete in the right direction so far as appreciating the fact that different literary forms demand different reading strategies.

201 W. A. Beardslee. *Literary Criticism of the New Testament*. GBS. Philadelphia: Fortress, 1970.

> A perplexing volume, in that it seems to confuse the old sense of literary or form criticism with the new sense as

it is used in English and literature departments. The results are not particularly helpful.

202 M. Boucher. *The Mysterious Parable.* Washington, D.C.:
Catholic Biblical Association, 1977.
Approach to the parables from a literary perspective.

203 R. A. Culpepper. *Anatomy of the Fourth Gospel: A Study in
Literary Design.* FF. Philadelphia: Fortress, 1983.
Still one of the better literary treatments, since it sticks
for the most part to a formal analysis (narrator, point of
view, plot, character). The chapter on implicit commentary is provocative, and the chapter on the implied reader
is one of the better chapters in the disappointingly exe-
cuted field of reader-response criticism.

204 P. Danove. *The End of Mark's Story: A Methodological
Study.* BIS 3. Leiden: Brill, 1993.
Perhaps undervalues the importance of historical setting
more than is warranted. Challenging method.

205 R. Detweiler. *Story, Sign, and Self: Phenomenology and
Structuralism as Literary Critical Methods.* SBLSS. Philadelphia: Fortress/Missoula: Scholars Press, 1978.
Good exposition of structuralism and phenomenology,
one that while recognizing their points of conflict holds
out the hope of profitable reconciliation as literary-criti-
cal methods.

206 P. Duke. *Irony in the Fourth Gospel.* Philadelphia: Fortress,
1986.
Simple but useful.

207 R. M. Fowler. *Let the Reader Understand: Reader-Response
Criticism and the Gospel of Mark.* Minneapolis: Fortress,
1991.
A recent exposition of reader-response criticism by one of
the tried and true advocates of the method. Fowler seems
to understand better than most what is going on (or not)
with this method.

208 H. W. Frei. *The Eclipse of Biblical Narrative: A Study in
Eighteenth and Nineteenth Century Hermeneutics.* New
Haven/London: Yale University Press, 1974.

Frei's classic study illustrates the transformation of values that occurred in the eighteenth and nineteenth centuries regarding the understanding of narrative, especially as applied to the biblical text. Not easy reading (more because of Frei's style than anything), it is nevertheless important to consider the pattern Frei observes for exegesis of narrative.

209 N. Frye. *The Great Code: The Bible and Literature.* New York/London: Harcourt, Brace, Jovanovich/London: Routledge and Kegan Paul, 1982.

Frye is one of few actual literary critics to analyze the Bible seriously. Not always convincing, but frequently challenging. Frye's reputation for exploring the concept of myth is exemplified here.

210 R. W. Funk. *The Poetics of Biblical Narrative.* Sonoma, Calif.: Polebridge, 1988.

A semilinguistic, formalist, and structuralist attempt to analyze narrative, concentrating on Mark. Difficult to understand and difficult to use.

211 K. R. R. Gros Louis et al. (eds.). *Literary Interpretations of Biblical Narratives.* 2 vols. Nashville: Abingdon, 1974, 1982.

When the first volume appeared, it was one of the first to explore literary readings of the Bible (most essays are on the Old Testament). When the second volume appeared it was not quite so novel, hence the fairly naive formalism does not produce many new insights.

212 P. J. Hartin and J. H. Petzer (eds.). *Text and Interpretation: New Approaches in the Criticism of the New Testament.* Leiden: Brill, 1991.

Included in this collection are essays by J. G. Du Plessis on speech act theory (pp. 129–42) and B. C. Lategan on reception theory (pp. 145–70) among others. Valuable approach.

213 D. Jasper. *The New Testament and the Literary Imagination.* Atlantic Highlands, N.J.: Humanities Press/London: Macmillan, 1987.

Good on generalities and provocative language, but not so good on exegesis.

214 F. Kermode. *The Genesis of Secrecy: On the Interpretation of Narrative.* Cambridge: Harvard University Press, 1979.
Kermode has made an important contribution to biblical studies, this being perhaps the most significant. He attempts to break out of the categories used by biblical scholars with regard to historical questions and explore Mark as narrative.

215 B. C. Lategan and W. S. Vorster. *Text and Reality: Aspects of Reference in Biblical Texts.* Atlanta: Scholars Press, 1985.
Four short but reasonable attempts to defend reception theory and reader-response theory by the authors. Many of the conclusions sound a lot like traditional literary observations, but they may still be important for just that reason.

216 T. Longman III. *Literary Approaches to Biblical Interpretation.* FCI 3. Grand Rapids: Zondervan/Leicester: InterVarsity, 1987.
A fine introduction to literary criticism (though focused mostly on the Old Testament). Hesitant to call into question various historically-based criteria.

217 E. V. McKnight. *Post-Modern Use of the Bible: The Emergence of Reader-Oriented Criticism.* Nashville: Abingdon, 1988.
What is postmodernism? After reading this text, you will still ask the same question but it is an interesting read.

218 E. V. McKnight. *The Bible and the Reader: An Introduction to Literary Criticism.* Philadelphia: Fortress, 1985.
Although brief, a fine conspectus of many of the major schools of thought in twentieth-century literary criticism. Reading a book like this will not make one a literary critic. You will still need to read the original texts as well.

219 E. V. McKnight and E. S. Malbon (eds.). *The New Literary Criticism and the New Testament.* JSNTSup 109. Sheffield: JSOT Press, 1994.

A fine collection of essays—some very interesting—but not a very representative survey of current discussion.

220 S. D. Moore. *Literary Criticism and the Gospels: The Theoretical Challenge.* New Haven/London: Yale University Press, 1989.

Moore's insightful book poses a serious challenge to many new literary critics, arguing that much of what they are doing is not particularly new or literary. In Moore's eyes much traditional criticism, such as redaction criticism, is more useful for understanding the literary dimensions of the text.

221 S. D. Moore. *Mark and Luke in Poststructuralist Perspectives: Jesus Begins to Write.* New Haven/London: Yale University Press, 1992.

A Joycian event. Very clever, but is it useful? Perhaps a good indication of where poststructuralist criticism has gone. See now Moore's *Poststructuralism and the New Testament: Derrida and Foucault at the Foot of the Cross.* Minneapolis: Fortress, 1994.

222 N. R. Petersen. *Literary Criticism for New Testament Critics.* GBS. Philadelphia: Fortress, 1978.

Petersen distances literary criticism from traditional historical criticism, and then utilizes a model based upon the linguist-semiotician R. Jakobson's communications model, with application to Mark. A good introduction.

223 L. M. Poland. *Literary Criticism and Biblical Hermeneutics: A Critique of Formalist Approaches.* AARAS 48. Chico: Scholars Press, 1985.

An important study that sought to clarify the implications of formalist approaches to interpretation.

224 S. E. Porter. "Why Hasn't Reader-Response Criticism Caught on in New Testament Studies?" *Literature and Theology* 4 (1990) 278–92.

A critique of so-called reader-response criticism.

225 M. A. Powell. *What is Narrative Criticism? A New Approach to the Bible.* Minneapolis: Fortress, 1990/London: SPCK, 1993.

Powell's attempt to justify so-called narrative criticism as a particularly and uniquely biblically oriented literary method of analysis. Not very convincing, since the approach can hardly be called new.

226 D. Rhoads and D. Michie. *Mark as Story: An Introduction to the Narrative of a Gospel.* Philadelphia: Fortress, 1982.

One of the first literary treatments of the New Testament, and one that has been imitated (and copied) much since. The approach is essentially formalist, concerned with such things as the narrative voice, setting, plot, and character. Even though Mark is analyzed, there is enough general discussion to get a sense of the categories.

227 D. Seeley. *Deconstructing the New Testament.* BIS 5. Leiden: Brill, 1994.

It is unclear where deconstruction as an interpretive strategy in New Testament studies will go. On the basis of this book, not far, since what is presented is more like traditional criticism with a new terminology. The readings are often traditional.

228 M. W. G. Stibbe. *John as Storyteller: Narrative Criticism and the Fourth Gospel.* SNTSMS 73. Cambridge: Cambridge University Press, 1992.

An attempt to integrate literary, structural, sociological, and historical criticism, hence bridging the gap that threatens to divide. The individual treatments are pretty brief.

229 M. A. Talbert. *Perspectives on the Parables.* Philadelphia: Fortress, 1979.

Literary treatment of the parables.

230 D. O. Via, Jr. *The Parables: Their Literary and Existential Dimension.* Philadelphia: Fortress, 1967.

Literary treatment of the parables. Lacks detail.

231 E. M. Wainwright. *Towards a Feminist Critical Reading of the Gospel according to Matthew.* Beihefte zur ZNW 60. Berlin/New York: de Gruyter, 1991.

An example of a feminist perspective. Far from convincing.

232 A. N. Wilder. *The Bible and the Literary Critic.* Minneapolis: Fortress, 1991.

Reprints of a number of recent essays, in all a disparate collection but one that attests to the importance of the work of the late poetic scholar Amos Wilder. If the approach of some of the essays seems dated, one can also acknowledge that Wilder was giving literary readings before many of the new breed of literary critics were born.

Rhetorical Criticism

Rhetorical criticism attracts much attention these days. Although it has been tried on the Old Testament, its productive capacity has been much higher for the New Testament, especially the writings of Paul. The approaches demonstrated are at least three. There are those who follow the work of G. A. Kennedy (see nos. 234, 235), the classical scholar who has done more to revive interest in classical rhetoric than any other. His contention is that rhetorical principles were simply a part of the culture and literary environment of the Greco-Roman world, and that the New Testament writers would have known the basic principles almost instinctively. Others follow the work of H. D. Betz (see no. 754), who makes rhetorical accomplishment much more of a planned thing in direct imitation of the classical handbooks. Paul ends up looking like a formal student of rhetoric. The third group follows the work of W. Wuellner (see nos. 245, 246), who follows the work of C. Perelman. The contention is that rhetoric constitutes a set of universals by which anyone, ancient or modern, constructs a persuasive argument. These principles are embedded in any argumentative writing and are susceptible to rhetorical analysis. There are New Testament rhetorical critics who have followed each of these schools of thought, but not without attracting various forms of criticism. The critical debate is becoming more intense as some begin to realize that rhetoric is not the solution to all interpretive problems. Rhetorical criticism can be found in a number of recent commentaries, including especially those by Wanamaker (no. 773) and Longenecker (no. 761).

233 B. Fiore. *The Function of Personal Example in the Socratic and Pastoral Epistles.* Analecta Biblica 105. Rome: Pontifical Biblical Institute, 1986.

Comparison of two forms of letters, claiming to find similarities in the use of personal examples.

234 G. A. Kennedy. *New Testament Interpretation through Rhetorical Criticism.* Chapel Hill/London: University of North Carolina Press, 1984.

A very significant though brief study of classical rhetorical criticism as applied to the New Testament. A school of thought has formed around Kennedy's approach, seen in recent commentaries by Longenecker on Galatians (no. 761) and Wanamaker on 1 and 2 Thessalonians (no. 773), besides a number of other studies.

235 G. A. Kennedy. *Classical Rhetoric and its Christian and Secular Tradition from Ancient to Modern Times.* Chapel Hill: University of North Carolina Press, 1980.

Brief potted histories of the development of rhetoric from its Homeric origins through the classical rhetoricians and on into the Christian period. Kennedy finds a thread that weaves them all together. Kennedy's most important work is *The Art of Persuasion in Greece.* Princeton: Princeton University Press, 1963. He has now done an important translation, *Aristotle On Rhetoric: A Theory of Civic Discourse.* New York/Oxford: Oxford University Press, 1991.

236 D. Litfin. *St. Paul's Theology of Proclamation: 1 Corinthians 1–4 and Greco-Roman Rhetoric.* SNTSMS 79. Cambridge: Cambridge University Press, 1994.

Litfin's four chapters on Greco-Roman rhetoric are very useful for tracing the development of rhetoric into the first century. His understanding of Paul's relationship to rhetoric is a bit more suspect. It also seems as if his work is a little dated, since he is still fighting against those who think that rhetoric is simply verbal legerdemain.

237 G. Lyons. *Pauline Autobiography: Toward a New Understanding.* SBLDS 73. Atlanta: Scholars Press, 1985.

Lyons discusses the use of autobiography in the ancient world in his opening chapter (pp. 17–73). Is he convincing? Perhaps there is a bit too much of modern categories at play here.

238 B. L. Mack. *Rhetoric and the New Testament.* GBS. Minneapolis: Fortress, 1990.

A basic introduction with history of research, basic classical theory, and some application to the New Testament. Mack assumes the validity of the categories, but does not argue for them. Overall a little disappointing.

239 B. L. Mack and V. K. Robbins. *Patterns of Persuasion in the Gospels.* FF. Sonoma, Calif.: Polebridge, 1989.

More—much more—on the *chreia* and related items. Perhaps more than anybody really wants.

240 M. M. Mitchell. *Paul and the Rhetoric of Reconciliation: An Exegetical Investigation of the Language and Composition of 1 Corinthians.* HUT 28. Tübingen: Mohr-Siebeck, 1991.

The best Betz treatment yet, although based on a fundamental logical and linguistic flaw, and reductionistic regarding explaining the Corinthian situation.

241 S. E. Porter and T. H. Olbricht (eds.). *Rhetoric and the New Testament: Essays from the 1992 Heidelberg Conference.* JSNTSup 90. Sheffield: JSOT Press, 1993.

A significant collection of essays on rhetoric, including a number that discuss questions of method, such as what does it mean to say that Paul was a rhetorician. Contributors to this theoretical discussion include C. J. Classen, S. E. Porter, J. T. Reed, and D. L. Stamps. Other essays are by such notables in rhetorical studies as V. K. Robbins, D. F. Watson, and W. Wuellner.

242 M. Warner (ed.). *The Bible as Rhetoric: Studies in Biblical Persuasion and Credibility.* Warwick Studies in Philosophy and Literature. London/New York: Routledge, 1990.

Some interesting essays that explore the persuasive power of the biblical texts. The Perelman idea of universal rhetoric provides the basic model for the essays.

243 D. F. Watson (ed.). *Persuasive Artistry: Studies in New Testament Rhetoric in Honor of G. A. Kennedy.* JSNTSup 50. Sheffield: JSOT Press, 1991.

One of the first volumes devoted to application of rhetorical studies to the New Testament. A useful collection, although not as methodologically self-conscious as one might want, except for the essay by J. R. Levison, which reflects on the development of Kennedy's own thought.

244 D. F. Watson and A. J. Hauser. *Rhetorical Criticism of the Bible: A Comprehensive Bibliography with Notes on History and Method.* BIS 4. Leiden: Brill, 1994.

Watson's comments on history and method (pp. 101–25) provide a useful survey of the field, especially where he notes the differences in method between using Greco-Roman rhetoric and modern rhetoric.

245 W. Wuellner. "Where is Rhetorical Criticism Taking Us?" *CBQ* 49 (1987) 448–63.

A review of the field from Wuellner's perspective and a plea for more work in it. Apparently the plea was successful.

246 W. Wuellner. "Hermeneutics and Rhetorics: From 'Truth and Method' to 'Truth and Power.'" *Scriptura S* 3 (1989) 1–54.

The best exposition and defense of Wuellner's rhetorical model, which is dependent upon C. Perelman. The thesis is that the categories of rhetoric are universals utilized in a range of discourse for persuasive means. Rhetoric is not simply a phenomenon of the past or one understood only through ancient categories, although Wuellner ties them all together.

7

Social-Scientific Criticism

Social-scientific criticism is one of the more recent methods to make its way into New Testament studies. In one sense, social description of early Christianity is something that has been done for two centuries (e.g., F. C. Baur, A. Deissmann, F. C. Grant, and other scholars who attempted to describe the people of the early church) and was even part of the form-critical agenda early on. But in a more technical sense social studies of the New Testament are only about twenty-five years old. Social-scientific studies can be divided into two rough-and-ready categories, those doing social description and those doing social analysis or sociology proper. Of course the two are interactive, but they generally describe those who offer classifications of the social data and those who utilize a model from sociology to describe the social scene. Within these two categories there are many different approaches as well, just as within sociology there are a number of interpretive models being utilized. One of the shortcomings of social science criticism of the New Testament is that many of those practicing it are not actually sociologists. As those with more sociological training enter the discipline the results are bound to grow. Other studies that address sociological issues are listed in the section on Greco-Roman backgrounds (see Part 3, chapter 13).

7.1 Introductions

247 J. H. Elliott. *What is Social-Scientific Criticism?* GBS. Minneapolis: Fortress, 1993.

Excellent bibliography. Probably too optimistic (and more than a little defensive) regarding the potential of social-scientific method. See his detailed study (no. 261).

248 P. F. Esler. *The First Christians in their Social Worlds: Social-Scientific Approaches to New Testament Interpretation.* London/New York: Routledge, 1994.

Esler's book is less about various social-scientific approaches than it is about how he as a sociological analyst responds to nonsociological approaches. He demonstrates his approach in terms of several different kinds of texts, including several chapters on apocalyptic material. See also his *Community and Gospel in Luke–Acts: The Social and Political Motivation of Lucan Theology.* SNTSMS 57. Cambridge: Cambridge University Press, 1987.

249 B. Holmberg. *Sociology and the New Testament: An Appraisal.* Minneapolis: Fortress, 1990.

Probably the best survey of scholarship of the last twenty years that brings sociology to bear on New Testament study, with particular though certainly not exclusive attention to European writers. He discusses in particular the debate over social levels of early Christians, as well as millenarian movements and sociology of knowledge. See his major study (no. 263).

250 C. Osiek. *What Are They Saying about the Social Setting of the New Testament?* New York/Mahwah, N.J.: Paulist, 1984. Revised edition: 1992.

A brief survey of major topics, as well as major works in the area, with emphasis upon social description. Included is a helpful annotated bibliography of work in the area.

251 P. J. Richter. "Recent Sociological Approaches to the Study of the New Testament." *Religion* 14 (1984) 77–90.

Arguably the most comprehensive classification of recent work by one trained in both sociology and New Testament. Differentiates between protosociological work and sociology proper (not all are happy with this terminology).

252 J. J. Pilch and B. J. Malina (eds.). *Biblical Social Values and their Meaning: A Handbook*. Peabody: Hendrickson, 1993.

A collection of short alphabetically arranged essays on various sociologically related topics. The tendency is to make the Mediterranean world of ancient times seem very different and remote from the modern world, falling victim to a number of unwarranted disjunctions and reductionistic thinking.

253 D. Tidball. *The Social Context of the New Testament: A Sociological Analysis*. Grand Rapids: Zondervan, 1984. British edition: *An Introduction to the Sociology of the New Testament*. Exeter: Paternoster, 1983.

A brief but useful though elementary survey of work in the area of sociology from a fairly conservative standpoint.

7.2 Technical Analyses

The following two categories are meant simply to provide a means of access to the two major categories of discussion, those who seek to describe on the basis of the New Testament and related data the world of the early Christians and those who approach the same topic by means of sociological models. In the first category tend to be the earlier studies, in the second tend to be the more recent studies that are more avowedly methodologically based. This is not to say that one category necessarily lists the more convincing discussions. Neither is it to say that others would not put the same discussions into other categories.

7.2.1 Social Description

254 M. Hengel. *Property and Riches in the Early Church: Aspects of a Social History of Early Christianity*. Translated by J. Bowden. Philadelphia: Fortress/London: SCM, 1974. Original title: *Eigentum und Reichtum in der frühen Kirche*. Stuttgart: Calwer, 1973. Reprinted in *Earliest Christianity*. Philadelphia: Fortress/London: SCM, 1986.

Hengel attempts to bridge the gap between early attitudes toward property and riches and contemporary attitudes. Hengel assesses a voluntary communal spirit toward possessions in the early church. Many of Hengel's studies would fall into the category of social description,

such as *Judaism and Hellenism* (see nos. 348/482, 349).
Valuable resource.

255 R. F. Hock. *The Social Context of Paul's Ministry: Tent-making and Apostleship.* Philadelphia: Fortress, 1980.

A brief but well-argued study regarding the social and economic context of Paul's tentmaking, as well as discussion of how this figures with Paul's unwillingness to accept support from his churches. Paul is seen to originate from a relatively high social level.

256 E. A. Judge. *The Social Pattern of Christian Groups in the First Century.* London: Tyndale, 1960.

One of the first and in some ways still one of the best sociological descriptions of Christianity in the first century, by an acknowledged master of ancient history. Departed significantly from the dominating views of A. Deissmann.

257 A. J. Malherbe. *Social Aspects of Early Christianity.* Baton Rouge/London: Louisiana State University Press, 1977. Second edition: Philadelphia: Fortress, 1983.

Malherbe presents several brief but insightful essays on the social, cultural, and linguistic background of Christianity, including social levels and the house-church movement (he departs from A. Deissmann's analysis). He sees a diversity in the composition of the early church, making it fit well within Greco-Roman society. In some ways a further development of Judge (see no. 256). The second edition brings the survey of research up to date.

258 J. Stambaugh and D. Balch. *The New Testament in its Social Environment.* LEC 2. Philadelphia: Westminster/London: SPCK, 1986.

A good introduction to social description, including discussions of the various economic classes in the ancient world and their relationship to the New Testament, as well as discussion of urban life.

259 G. Theissen. *Sociology of Early Palestinian Christianity.* Translated by J. Bowden. Philadelphia: Fortress, 1978. British edition: *The First Followers of Jesus.* London: SCM, 1978. Original title: *Soziologie der Jesusbewegung: Ein Bei-*

trag zur Entstehungsgeschichte des Urchristentums. Munich: Kaiser, 1977.

Simplified, if not simplistic, account of early Christianity. Tends to make it look like a group of lower-class followers. See R. A. Horsley. *Sociology and the Jesus Movement.* New York: Crossroad, 1989. Reprinted: New York: Continuum, 1994, for a critical response, rejecting Theissen's functionalist model for his own that relies upon social stratification.

260 G. Theissen. *The Shadow of the Galilean: The Quest of the Historical Jesus in Narrative Form.* Translated by J. Bowden. Philadelphia: Fortress/London: SCM, 1987. Original title: *Der Schatten des Galiläers: Historische Jesusforschung in erzählender Form.* Munich: Kaiser, 1986.

Raises important questions for Life-of-Jesus research. Not all will be convinced by his answers.

7.2.2 Sociology Proper

261 J. H. Elliott. *A Home for the Homeless: A Social-Scientific Criticism of 1 Peter, its Situation and Strategy.* Philadelphia: Fortress/London: SCM, 1981. Revised edition: Minneapolis: Fortress, 1990.

An often-cited study in establishing the agenda for much social-scientific work, although the new preface that responds to criticism is more an effort in self-justification than coming to terms with charges regarding reductionism and failure to consider the range of ancient evidence. Significant influence on studies by P. Esler, E. MacDonald, and F. Watson.

262 J. G. Gager. *Kingdom and Community: The Social World of Early Christianity.* Englewood Cliffs, N.J.: Prentice-Hall, 1975.

An early and influential sociologically based study using cognitive dissonance theory, but one that has been severely criticized for the sociological models it uses.

263 B. Holmberg. *Paul and Power: The Structure of Authority in the Primitive Church as Reflected in the Pauline Epistles.* Coniectanea Biblica. Lund: Gleerup, 1978/Philadelphia: Fortress, 1980.

This study of levels and relationships of power in the early church concentrates upon Paul, but has wider application. The theories of Max Weber are seen to be important in discussing these social structures.

264 R. A. Horsley with J. S. Hanson. *Bandits, Prophets, and Messiahs: Popular Movements at the Time of Jesus.* San Francisco: Harper & Row, 1985.

The authors attempt to bring social-scientific methodology to bear on understanding the long-neglected popular and populist movements of Palestine, those who have traditionally been neglected, mischaracterized, or misunderstood regarding their significance. Significant contribution.

265 H. C. Kee. *Christian Origins in Sociological Perspective.* Philadelphia: Westminster/London: SCM, 1980.

An overview of the major social categories to consider in analyzing the New Testament, although it appears that the author must work pretty hard for not much gain in several instances.

266 H. C. Kee. *Knowing the Truth: Sociological Approach to New Testament Interpretation.* Minneapolis: Fortress, 1989.

Recognizes the tension between imposing sociological models or giving sociological description.

267 B. J. Malina. *The New Testament World: Insights from Cultural Anthropology.* Atlanta: John Knox/London: SCM, 1981.

Often regarded as a standard example of a social-scientific approach to the New Testament (some would clearly differentiate anthropology from sociology). Many of the explanations do nothing more than distance us unnecessarily from the ancient world. Especially questionable are discussions of honor and shame and of first-century personality. See also his *Christian Origins and Cultural Anthropology: Practical Models for Biblical Interpretation.* Atlanta: John Knox, 1986.

268 B. J. Malina and R. L. Rohrbaugh. *Social-Science Commentary on the Synoptic Gospels.* Minneapolis: Fortress, 1992.

A brief commentary on the Gospels treated individually, with interspersed references to more extensive essays on sociologically relevant topics. The essays are not always as incisive as one might wish, calling into question how much payoff there really is in some social-scientific criticism.

269 W. A. Meeks. *The First Urban Christians: The Social World of the Apostle Paul.* New Haven/London: Yale University Press, 1983.

Investigation of the Pauline churches from the standpoint of the urban world in which they were located. This has established itself as one of the crucial studies to consider when assessing the Pauline mission. Not only does it go beyond Judge and Malherbe, but many would say that it is methodologically sounder.

270 W. A. Meeks. *The Moral World of the First Christians.* LEC 6. Philadelphia: Westminster, 1986/London: SCM, 1987.

An exploration of the symbolic world of the first Christians, attempting to show those areas both in which Christianity was new, and in which it perpetuated existing traditions of the various worlds (Greek and Semitic) of which it was a part. This was one of the first studies to try to construct a full picture of the social world of early Christianity, appreciating especially the Greco-Roman influence.

271 J. Neyrey (ed.). *The Social World of Luke–Acts: Models for Interpretation.* Peabody: Hendrickson, 1991.

A collection of papers from a sociological standpoint and applied to Luke–Acts. The emphases are upon the basic societal institutions, the psychology of sociology, and the various means by which culture is mediated. Some of it is pretty superficial and some is substantial. Neyrey has written a commentary from a social-science perspective (see no. 791).

272 N. R. Petersen. *Rediscovering Paul: Philemon and the Sociology of Paul's Narrative World.* Philadelphia: Fortress, 1985.

This literary and sociological study is incredibly insightful. Philemon is a perfect text for examination, in which Petersen develops highly useful categories regarding narrative and the actual world, from which he reconstructs the social relations of the letter.

273 G. Theissen. *The Social Setting of Pauline Christianity: Essays on Corinth.* Translated by J. Schütz. Philadelphia: Fortress/Edinburgh: T. & T. Clark, 1982.

This volume is a collection of essays first published individually in German. What unifies them is Theissen's perspective, in which he concentrates upon social, cultural, and economic issues in the legitimation of Paul as an apostle and behind the various conflicts in Corinth.

274 G. Theissen. *Social Reality and the Early Christians: Theology, Ethics, and the World of the New Testament.* Translated by M. Kohl. Minneapolis: Augsburg, 1992/Edinburgh: T. & T. Clark, 1993.

Of particular interest is the first chapter, which traces the rise and fall and reemergence of sociological exegesis. The rest of the book is divided into two parts, the first concerned with Jesus tradition and the second with Paul. There is much useful social-scientific analysis here (avoiding most instances of forced categories), applied to theological and ethical issues. His analysis of early Christianity is in broad agreement with Judge and Meeks.

275 C. P. Rowland and M. Corner. *Liberating Exegesis: The Challenge of Liberation Theology to Biblical Studies.* Louisville: Westminster/John Knox/London: SPCK, 1989.

The challenge of the difference liberation theology makes to sound exegesis is still with us, but the authors are at least to be commended for trying to illustrate the relationship of the two.

Structuralism

Structuralism as a method for interpreting texts apparently has waned in interest, despite the best efforts of one or two scholars to keep the area alive. Several important questions are raised by structuralist approaches, questions whose answers have had enduring value in how they have influenced other methods of interpretation (social-scientific criticism, literary criticism, etc.). Structuralism has apparently had more productive interpretive capacity in Old Testament rather than New Testament studies. In New Testament studies it appears to have been used most profitably in interpretation of the parables. Several major questions confronted structuralism from the start: Was it a heuristic tool or a complete value-laden worldview? What status did "structures" have, were they merely interpretive constructs or actual universal structures? Was the method being reductionistic in claiming to be able to analyze all narratives according to a set number of structural patterns? In the end, it appears that the readings offered were not provocative enough to generate continuing widespread interest.

276 J. D. Crossan (ed.). *The Good Samaritan. Semeia* 2. Missoula: Scholars Press, 1974.

> A classic collection of essays exposing the strengths and weaknesses of structural exegesis as applied to one text. Contributors include Crossan, D. Patte, R. W. Funk, R. C.

Tannehill, D. O. Via, Jr., A. N. Wilder, and W. G. Doty. See also *Semeia* 1. Missoula: Scholars Press, 1974.

277 D. C. Greenwood. *Structuralism and the Biblical Text.* New York/Amsterdam: Mouton, 1985.

A review and critique of work in structuralism applied to the Bible.

278 A. M. Johnson, Jr. (ed.). *Structuralism and Biblical Hermeneutics: A Collection of Essays.* Pittsburgh: Pickwick, 1979.

Included in this collection is R. Barthes's "A Structural Analysis of a Narrative from Acts X–XI" (pp. 109–44), among other essays.

279 B. W. Kovacs. "Philosophical Foundations for Structuralism." Pp. 85–105 in *Narrative Syntax: Translations and Reviews.* Edited by J. D. Crossan. *Semeia* 10. Chico: Scholars Press, 1978.

An important though difficult study regarding the basis of structuralism. It still remains one of the best statements for outlining the structural agenda. The entire issue of *Semeia* was devoted to structuralism.

280 E. V. McKnight. *Meaning in Texts: The Historical Shaping of a Narrative Hermeneutics.* Philadelphia: Fortress, 1978.

Structuralism defined and employed to analyze narrative. Long on description, especially of some of the major figures (e.g., M. Heidegger, W. Dilthey).

281 D. Patte. *What Is Structural Exegesis?* GBS. Philadelphia: Fortress, 1976.

A good, simple introduction to this subject, before it started to take itself too seriously and think that it could solve all interpretive problems. See also D. and A. Patte. *Structural Exegesis: From Theory to Practice—Exegesis of Mark 15 and 16, Hermeneutical Implications.* Philadelphia: Fortress, 1978, where a structural-semiotic theory is applied to two chapters in Mark.

282 D. Patte. *Structural Exegesis for New Testament Critics.* GBS. Minneapolis: Fortress, 1990.

To some extent a revision of Patte's first book in this same series (see no. 281), but in this one the method has become a mind-set, and one not shared by all. Patte has written commentaries on Matthew and Paul using his method of structural analysis.

283 D. Robey (ed.). *Structuralism: An Introduction.* Oxford: Oxford University Press, 1973.

An excellent introduction to structuralism as it is found in various disciplines, such as linguistics (J. Lyons, J. Culler), literary study (T. Todorov), anthropology (R. Leech), semiotics (U. Eco), and others.

284 R. A. Spencer (ed.). *Orientation by Disorientation: Studies in Literary Criticism and Biblical Literary Criticism in Honour of W. A. Beardslee.* Pittsburgh: Pickwick, 1980.

Included in this collection are essays by J. D. Crossan, "A Structuralist Analysis of John 6" (pp. 235–49) and others.

285 A. C. Thiselton. "Structuralism and Biblical Studies: Method or Ideology?" *ExpTim* 89 (1978) 329–35.

An examination of some of the important theoretical and methodological questions relating to structuralism.

286 D. O. Via, Jr. *Kerygma and Comedy in the New Testament: A Structuralist Approach to Hermeneutic.* Philadelphia: Fortress, 1975.

Analysis of Paul and Mark using structuralist method.

History of New Testament Interpretation

A feature of understanding the New Testament that has not always been fully appreciated is the history of its interpretation. Knowing the history of interpretation can be beneficial in several ways, including helping to avoid interpretive mistakes of the past, making us realize that interpretation occurs at the end of a process, and placing any interpretation within a cultural, historical, linguistic, and theological context. There are several kinds of histories of interpretation available that range from simple recountings to detailed examinations.

287 W. Baird. *History of New Testament Research.* I. *From Deism to Tübingen.* Minneapolis: Fortress, 1992.

> Traces the history of modern criticism through to F. C. Baur and mediating responses to him. There is plenty of description, summary of authors, and illustrative quotations. Probably the best book of its kind, though not easy reading.

288 W. G. Doty. *Contemporary New Testament Interpretation.* Englewood Cliffs, N.J.: Prentice-Hall, 1972.

> A study of recent trends up to the time of writing. Some good insights but awfully brief.

289 R. M. Grant. *A Short History of the Interpretation of the Bible*. London: Macmillan, 1963. Second edition with D. Tracy: Philadelphia: Fortress/London: SPCK, 1984.

A short history of interpretation with an appended theological postscript. The topics are not always evenly handled and certainly not complete, but the volume gives an overview of the broad sweep of interpretation. Still a valuable contribution.

290 P. Henry. *New Directions in New Testament Study*. Philadelphia: Westminster, 1979/London: SCM, 1980.

Summary of recent research regarding such things as Jewish background, gnosticism, historical Jesus, Paul, and the like. Obviously from a perspective.

291 W. G. Kümmel. *The New Testament: The History of the Investigation of its Problems*. Translated by S. McL. Gilmour and H. C. Kee. Nashville/New York: Abingdon, 1972. Original title: *Das Neue Testament: Geschichte der Erforschung seiner Probleme*. Karl Alber, 1970.

With emphasis upon the Continental, especially German, contribution to New Testament scholarship, Kümmel illustrates by means of significant quotations from the authors. There are some notable omissions such as J. H. Moulton, W. Ramsay, and an obvious rivalry with his English counterpart, S. Neill (see no. 294), nevertheless, a very important contribution and basic reader for all interested in the field.

292 J. L. Kugel and R. A. Greer. *Early Biblical Interpretation*. LEC 3. Philadelphia: Westminster, 1986.

Traces the development of biblical interpretation into the early church period, with Greer giving emphasis to the Fathers.

293 R. Morgan with J. Barton. *Biblical Interpretation*. OBS. Oxford: Oxford University Press, 1988.

The most up-to-date history of the rise of modern biblical interpretation, including the two more recent approaches of social-scientific analysis and literary interpretation. Although there are some interesting quirks of analysis, the extended references to important scholarly works are excellent.

294 S. C. Neill. *The Interpretation of the New Testament 1861–1961*. Oxford: Oxford University Press, 1964. Second edition: *The Interpretation of the New Testament 1861–1986* revised by N. T. Wright: 1988.

An outstanding survey of research by Neill, who was for the most part amazingly astute in his judgments. Wright tries to bring the book up to date but has neither Neill's style nor acumen, neglecting several of the more important developments of the last twenty-five years.

295 J. K. Riches. *A Century of New Testament Study*. Cambridge: Lutterworth, 1993.

A brief and in many ways selective and idiosyncratic account of the development of New Testament study over the last one hundred years. Neglected virtually completely are such topics as Greek language and linguistics, much social-scientific criticism, and virtually all of the recent developments in literary analysis. The Germans are given their due, but overall S. Neill (see no. 294) is still a better guide.

296 J. Rogerson, C. Rowland, and B. Lindars. *The Study and Use of the Bible*. The History of Christian Theology 2. Grand Rapids: Eerdmans/Basingstoke: Marshall Pickering, 1988.

Lindars writes on the New Testament. His potted summaries are very useful in establishing a quick foundation (although his isn't the best part of the volume).

Part 3

Historical Backgrounds

10

New Testament History and Times

Books in this category comprise necessary companions to introductions. Whereas the introduction is meant to emphasize the text of the New Testament, the history-and-times book is designed to establish the larger context. These volumes should be supplemented with even broader histories of the Greco-Roman world, mentioned in Part 3, chapter 13.2.2. History-and-times books vary much as do introductions. That is, they vary in the amount and kind of detail that they present. Some give a superficial accounting of the world of the New Testament, while others discuss various historical issues in more detail, often providing references to primary sources (see chapter 13.1 regarding primary texts). The major means of classifying them is whether they are concerned to offer a historical description of the world out of which the New Testament arose or whether they are concerned to account for the development of the New Testament in terms of various kinds of social or religious models.

The following works focus on the historical context of early Christianity. As histories, they do not generally focus on the literary development of the New Testament so much as the historical context that gave rise to the literature of the New Testament. That context is both Jewish and Greco-Roman and focuses on the competing philosophies and religious activity of the Jews and early Christian community from around the early second century

B.C. to the late second century A.D. In recent years there has been a variety of excellent literature produced in this field with which the careful interpreter of the New Testament will certainly become familiar.

297 W. Bauer. *Orthodoxy and Heresy in Earliest Christianity, with an Appendix by G. Strecker.* Edited by R. A. Kraft and G. Krodel. Philadelphia: Fortress, 1971. Original title: *Rechtgläubigkeit und Ketzerei im ältesten Christentum.* Tübingen: Mohr-Siebeck, 1934. Second edition: 1964.

A very influential book in the English-speaking world for recreating early Christianity. The argument is that early Christianity was highly diverse, making it difficult to define orthodoxy and heresy as single things. The development of orthodoxy ends up resembling the winning side in a struggle.

298 F. C. Baur. *The Church History of the First Three Centuries.* Translated by A. Menzies. 2 vols. London: Williams and Norgate, third edition, 1878. Original title: *Geschichte der Christlichen Kirche.* 3 vols. Tübingen: Mohr, second and third edition, 1862–69.

One of several significant works by the prime mover in the so-called Tübingen school. Baur raised many good questions, many of them inadequately answered at the time, and his legacy is still present in critical New Testament study. H. Harris has put the Tübingen school of thought in perspective in *The Tübingen School.* Oxford: Clarendon, 1975. Second edition: Grand Rapids: Baker/ Leicester: InterVarsity, 1990.

299 F. F. Bruce. *New Testament History.* London: Nelson, 1969/ Garden City: Doubleday, 1971.

An outstanding resource of information without peer in its overall perspective. Shows familiarity with the Judaisms of the first century and the growth and development of early Christianity from the time of Jesus into the early second century. A conservative but highly reliable history of the New Testament, with attention paid to primary sources, including various nonbiblical texts. Bruce was expert on both the Jewish and Greco-Roman sides, which comes through in the book.

300 R. Bultmann. *Primitive Christianity in its Contemporary Setting.* Philadelphia: Fortress, 1956. Original title: *Das Urchristentum im Rahmen der antiken Religionen.* Zürich: Artemis, 1949.

Bultmann's attempt to reconstruct the origins of early Christianity, giving due emphasis to both Jewish and hellenistic dimensions, although few would put the balance where he does.

301 G. B. Caird. *The Apostolic Age.* London: Duckworth, 1955. Surveys history of early Christianity and the New Testament era in particular. Brief and helpful for the beginner, but lacking in detail and in discussion of the Jewish context. The advanced student will want something more substantial.

302 H. Conzelmann. *History of Primitive Christianity.* Translated by J. E. Steely. Nashville: Abingdon/London: Darton, Longman & Todd, 1973. Original title: *Geschichte des Urchristentums.* Göttingen: Vandenhoeck & Ruprecht.

A brief history of the development of the early church, from the teaching of Jesus to Jewish Christianity after the war of A.D. 70. Appended are a number of translated primary sources, essential reading for understanding many of the events of the early church. See no. 331.

303 E. Ferguson. *Backgrounds of Early Christianity.* Grand Rapids: Eerdmans, 1987. Second edition: 1993.

One of the finest works of its kind to appear in recent years. Describes fairly extensively both Jewish and Greco-Roman context of early Christianity, especially the historical. Second edition even more helpful and up-to-date. Conservative in detail but covering a broad spectrum of issues, philosophies, sects of Judaism and early Christianity, as well as the social context. Comprehensive and competent.

304 F. V. Filson. *A New Testament History: The Story of the Emerging Church.* Philadelphia: Westminster, 1964/London: SCM, 1965.

A readable history of the early church, still useful despite its age. Its focus is broad and traditional. Scholarship is evident and respect for the theological side of the New Testament is maintained throughout.

305 L. Goppelt. *Apostolic and Post-Apostolic Times.* Translated by R. A. Guelich. New York: Harper/London: A. & C. Black, 1970. Original title: *Die apostolische und nachapostolische Zeit.* Göttingen: Vandenhoeck & Ruprecht, 1962.

Plots the emergence of the church from its Jewish and Greco-Roman backgrounds, as well as considers its several internal struggles. Useful and informed discussion of the early Church and the issues that dominated its thinking in the first and early second century. Reliable, sane, and balanced, but the translation is not smooth and a bit too cryptic in places.

306 M. Goulder. *A Tale of Two Missions.* London: SCM, 1994.

The F. C. Baur hypothesis of two churches revived and strengthened (see no. 298). Goulder sees conflict from early on between Jerusalem (Peter and James) and Paul.

307 A. Harnack. *The Mission and Expansion of Christianity in the First Three Centuries.* Translated by J. Moffatt. London: Williams & Norgate, 1908.

One of the classic reconstructions of early Christianity, from a moderate German perspective.

308 J. N. D. Kelly. *Early Christian Doctrines.* San Francisco: Harper & Row/London: A. & C. Black, 1960. Fifth edition: 1978.

Kelly provides an excellent survey of Christian doctrine, focusing upon Christological controversies, by beginning in the pre-Christian period. The documentation of primary literature is superb, and to be considered when dealing with this topic.

309 E. Lohse. *The New Testament Environment.* Translated by J. E. Steely. Nashville: Abingdon/London: SCM, 1976. Original title: *Umwelt des Neuen Testaments.* Göttingen: Vandenhoeck & Ruprecht, second edition, 1974.

Although somewhat dated, still a useful text on the history of the Judaisms of the first century and the Greco-

Roman context of the early Christian movement, including the philosophies that the early Christians encountered in their missionary endeavors.

310 A. J. Malherbe. *Social Aspects of Early Christianity.* Baton Rouge/London: Louisiana State University Press, 1977. Second edition: Philadelphia: Fortress, 1983.

Brief but excellent resource on the social context of the early Christian community. Discusses the role of the house churches and the practice of hospitality. A solid contribution.

311 B. Reicke. *The New Testament Era: The World of the Bible from 500 B.C. to A.D. 100.* Translated by D. E. Green. Philadelphia: Fortress/London: A. & C. Black, 1968. Original title: *Neutestamentliche Zeitgeschichte.* Berlin: Töpelmann, 1964.

Excellent resource on the various movements and philosophies that were a part of the social milieu of early Christianity. Not as helpful on the Jewish background, but important focus on the Greek and Roman history and influences that affected early Christianity.

312 J. M. Robinson and H. Koester. *Trajectories through Early Christianity.* Philadelphia: Fortress, 1971.

A collection of essays by two authors who support W. Bauer's thesis of a plurality of traditions in early Christianity without a uniform development that led to "orthodoxy" in the second or even fourth century (see no. 297). A solid contribution that challenges many conservative views on the notion of theological development in the church.

313 A. Schlatter. *The Church in the New Testament Period.* Translated by P. P. Levertoff. London: SPCK, 1955. Original title: *Die Geschichte der ersten Christenheit.* Gütersloh: Bertelsmann, 1926.

Although dated, still an excellent resource for understanding early Christianity, especially its hellenistic context.

314 M. Tenney. *New Testament Times.* Grand Rapids: Eerdmans, 1965.

Although dated, a work that presents much of the historical material behind the New Testament, with reference to primary sources. The kind of detail that is really helpful is lacking, however.

11

New Testament Chronology

Chronological questions continue to be discussed in New Testament studies. The questions focus on two major areas: the dates surrounding the birth and crucifixion of Jesus Christ and the chronology and dating of Paul's missionary journeys. There has been long-standing debate about the date of Jesus' birth in relation to known and unknown events in the Roman Empire, and about the date of his death, including apparent internal problems between the Synoptic Gospels and John. Recent topics of dispute in establishing Pauline chronology revolve around the date of the edict of Claudius, where Paul's various missionary trips fit in relation to the Jerusalem Council, and how and whether Acts can be used in establishing a reliable chronology of the New Testament era.

315 C. J. Hemer. "Observations on Pauline Chronology." Pp. 3–18 in *Pauline Studies: Essays Presented to Professor F. F. Bruce on his 70th Birthday*. Edited by D. A. Hagner and M. J. Harris. Grand Rapids: Eerdmans/Exeter: Paternoster, 1980.
> An excellent statement of the traditional Pauline chronology.

316 H. W. Hoehner. *Chronological Aspects of the Life of Christ*. Grand Rapids: Zondervan, 1977.
> Conservative but adequate survey. Wrestles with important issues.

317 R. Jewett. *A Chronology of Paul's Life*. Philadelphia: Fortress, 1979. British edition: *Dating Paul's Life*. London: SCM, 1979.

Carefully written and worth the price.

318 J. Knox. *Chapters in a Life of Paul*. Nashville: Abingdon, 1950. Revised by D. R. A. Hare: Macon, Ga.: Mercer University Press, 1987/London: SCM, 1989.

Knox caused quite a stir when he proposed that Acts not be used to formulate a Pauline chronology, a conclusion that has divided those who try to establish Pauline chronology.

319 G. Luedemann. *Paul, Apostle to the Gentiles: Studies in Chronology*. Translated by F. S. Jones. Philadelphia: Fortress, 1984. Original title: *Paulus, der Heidenapostel*. I. *Studien zur Chronologie*. FRLANT 123. Göttingen: Vandenhoeck & Ruprecht, 1980.

Luedemann argues for a Pauline mission to Greece before the Jerusalem conference, defends his view of the early date of the edict of Claudius, and rejects the use of Acts as a primary source for Pauline chronology.

320 G. Ogg. *The Chronology of the Life of Paul*. London: Epworth, 1968.

One of the first modern treatments and raises the important questions. The answers are mixed.

12

Jewish Context of Early Christianity

It is axiomatic to say that early Christianity came out of Judaism, but what was the social context in which the earliest Christians worshiped and ministered? That context was a Jewish one, but therein lies the problem. There were many competing Judaisms in the first century and it is not clear that in the time of Jesus any one of them held priority in the land of Israel. What were the various Jewish sects that made up the multiple strands of Judaism? How much did each one of them affect the early Christian community that probably drew converts from each of the sects, especially that of Pharisaism? Life of Jesus studies today focus heavily on the Jewishness of Jesus and much has been gleaned from these inquiries. It has not been uncommon for some scholars of the various Judaisms of antiquity to interpret Christianity in terms of the rabbinic Judaism that prevailed among the Jews in the second century and following, but it is not clear that the interpreter of the life of Jesus can uncritically accept events and circumstances that prevailed in the second century and claim that they also obtained in the first. Caution is needed here, but that does not take away from the fact that the "third questers" of the historical Jesus, that is, the new "wave" of Jesus scholars, have taken more seriously than those before them the Jewish context of early Christianity. Along with Philo, Qumran (the Dead Sea

Scrolls), and Josephus, the Mishnah, Tosephta, Sifre, and Talmudim, as well as the various rabbinic midrashim, are very important writings that often have a long history behind them, some reaching back into the New Testament times or before. The following sources, though highly selective, are illustrative of the significant work going on in this area not only by Jewish scholars, but also by competent Christian scholars as well.

12.1 Judaism of the First and Second Centuries: General Focus

321 P. S. Alexander (ed. and trans.). *Textual Sources for the Study of Judaism.* Textual Sources for the Study of Religion. Manchester: Manchester University Press, 1984.

> A careful introduction to the scripture and tradition of the Jews from antiquity to the present. Well documented. Not as much interaction with Christianity except in an adversarial way.

322 L. Baeck. *The Pharisees and Other Essays.* New York: Schocken, 1947. Second edition: 1966.

> An older work by a rabbi who interpreted not only the essence of Judaism in the time of Jesus, but specifically the sects of Judaism. Shows a clear understanding of the Judaism from which early Christianity emerged. The work is significantly dated but still of value. K. Stendahl's introduction helps to establish the context of the book and clarify the issues.

323 G. Boccaccini. *Middle Judaism: Jewish Thought, 300 B.C.E. to 200 C.E.* Minneapolis: Fortress, 1991.

> A valuable description of what Judaism is including whether Christianity can still be called a Judaism. Describes in detail the Judaism out of which the two dominant Judaisms emerge: Christianity and Rabbinic Judaism. Generously documented with many primary sources.

324 J. Bowker. *The Targums and Rabbinic Literature: An Introduction to Jewish Interpretations of Scripture.* Cambridge: Cambridge University Press, 1969.

Discussion of the importance of the Targums, with virtually a complete translation of Pseudo-Jonathan.

325 P. Blackman (ed.). *Mishnayot: Pointed Hebrew Text, English Translation, Introductions.* 6 vols. New York: Judaica Press, 1963–64. Second edition: 1990.
Standard edition.

326 R. H. Charles (ed.). *The Apocrypha and Pseudepigrapha of the Old Testament.* 2 vols. Oxford: Clarendon, 1913.
Until recently the standard work on the apocrypha and pseudepigrapha. Still has valuable historical and textual data and in some cases the translation is superior to more recent translations.

327 J. H. Charlesworth (ed.). *Jesus' Jewishness: Exploring the Place of Jesus in Early Judaism.* Shared Ground Among Jews and Christians: A Series of Explorations 2. New York: Crossroad/The American Interfaith Institute, 1991.
Essays by prominent Jewish and Christian scholars who want to underscore the fact of Jesus' Jewishness to help bridge the chasm between Christians and Jews that has existed since the early centuries. The anti-Judaistic sentiment in the New Testament is also the root of the anti-semitism that marred church history and cost so many lives of innocent persons. Frank and open focus on understanding Jesus within his Jewish environment.

328 J. H. Charlesworth (ed.). *The Old Testament Pseudepigrapha.* 2 vols. Garden City: Doubleday, 1983, 1985.
An excellent translation of the pseudepigrapha along with helpful notations and introductions that has largely taken the place of R. H. Charles's (no. 326) similar work.

329 J. H. Charlesworth. *The Pseudepigrapha and Modern Research.* Missoula: Scholars Press, 1976. Revised edition with Supplement: 1981.
Discusses value of this literature for understanding New Testament inquiry. Draws interesting implications for canon research.

330 S. J. D. Cohen. *From the Maccabees to the Mishnah.* LEC. Philadelphia: Westminster, 1987.

Examines history that gave rise to rabbinic Judaism and early Christianity from the second temple to the second century. Helpful parallels between Judaism and Christianity are drawn.

331 H. Conzelmann. *Gentiles–Jews–Christians: Polemics and Apologetics in the Greco-Roman Era.* Translated by M. E. Boring. Minneapolis: Fortress, 1992. Original title: *Heiden—Juden—Christen: Auseinandersetzungen in der Literatur der hellenisch-römischen Zeit.* Tübingen: Mohr-Siebeck, 1981.

Provides a scholarly guide to the relevant literature of formative Judaism and Christianity of the first centuries of the common era. Well documented with numerous footnotes and sane conclusions about the early Jewish-Christian dialogue and where it should be going today, namely, appreciation and dialogue without either side of the debate surrendering its theological moorings.

332 H. Danby (trans.). *The Mishnah.* Oxford: Clarendon, 1933.

Still the standard edition, even with J. Neusner's *The Mishnah: A New Translation.* New Haven/London: Yale University Press, 1988.

333 D. Daube. *The New Testament and Rabbinic Judaism.* London: Athlone Press, 1956.

Still important early study and worth reading.

334 W. D. Davies and L. Finkelstein (eds.). *The Cambridge History of Judaism.* II. *The Hellenistic Age.* Cambridge: Cambridge University Press, 1989.

Contributors include M. Hengel, J. Barr, N. Walter and the editors, among others. Although some of the articles are quite useful, a delay in publication means that some of them were already seriously dated by the time they appeared. The volume has been criticized for this and other reasons. For an interesting analysis of the early part of the period, see E. J. Bickerman. *The Jews in the Greek Age.* Cambridge: Harvard University Press, 1988.

335 J. D. G. Dunn. *The Partings of the Ways between Christianity and Judaism and their Significance for the Character of*

Christianity. Philadelphia: Trinity Press International/London: SCM, 1991.

Focuses on the factors that brought the separation between early Christianity and Judaism and how that influenced each religious community. A significant contribution.

336 J. D. G. Dunn (ed.). *Jews and Christians: The Parting of the Ways A.D. 70 to 135*. WUNT 66. Tübingen: Mohr-Siebeck, 1992.

A collection of essays pursuing the theme of the tensions that led to the separation of Christianity from Judaism. There are essays by P. Alexander, M. Goodman, M. Hengel, G. N. Stanton, J. McHugh, P. Stuhlmacher, J. Dunn, C. Rowland, A. Chester, W. Horbury, and J. N. Birdsall.

337 D. P. Efroymson, E. J. Fisher, and L. Klenicki (eds.). *Within Context: Essays on Jews and Judaism in the New Testament*. Michael Glazier Book. Collegeville, Minn.: Liturgical Press, 1993.

A collection of essays by several prominent scholars who offer a balanced picture of the Jews in the time of Jesus and during the writing of the New Testament.

338 I. Epstein (ed.). *The Babylonian Talmud*. 35 vols. London: Soncino, 1935–48. Reprint: 1961 in 18 vols.

Standard English edition.

339 C. A. Evans. *Noncanonical Writings and New Testament Interpretation*. Peabody: Hendrickson, 1992.

Offers a brief but reliable introduction and listing of the ancient literature that was not a part of the Christian biblical canon, but nevertheless circulated before, during, and after the emergence of early Christianity. There are useful introductions, discussions, and bibliographies of primary and secondary literature for the Old and New Testament apocrypha and pseudepigrapha, Dead Sea scrolls, Septuagint, Philo and Josephus, rabbinic literature, early church fathers, gnostic writings, and the papyri, plus a few others. Excellent resource for students and scholars.

340 E. Ferguson. *Backgrounds of Early Christianity.* Grand Rapids: Eerdmans, 1987. Second edition: 1993.

Arguably one of the best historical introductions to the social context of early Christianity. The second edition is essentially an update of the still valuable first edition and is a balanced and sane treatment of the Jewish and pagan context of early Christianity. One of the standard texts on the subject, though more detailed treatments are referred to in the bibliographies.

341 M. I. Finley (ed.). *Studies in Ancient Society.* Past and Present Series. London: Routledge and Kegan Paul, 1974.

Remarkable collection of essays by distinguished scholars focusing on the context of early Christianity and especially its Jewish context.

342 J. A. Fitzmyer. *Essays on the Semitic Background of the New Testament.* London: Geoffrey Chapman, 1971/Chico: Scholars Press, 1974.

Classic collection of Fitzmyer's essays, including those on the early Christian use of the Old Testament, the Semitic background of the New Testament, as well as his authoritative article on the Oxyrhynchus *logoi* of Jesus and Thomas (pp. 355–433).

343 J. A. Fitzmyer. *A Wandering Aramean: Collected Aramaic Essays.* SBLMS 25. Chico: Scholars Press, 1979.

A number of crucial essays regarding the linguistic background of the New Testament. Although Aramaic is discussed at greatest length, other languages are touched on as well.

344 W. Förster. *Palestinian Judaism in New Testament Times.* Translated by G. E. Harris. Edinburgh/London: Oliver & Boyd, 1965. Original title: *Neutestamentliche Zeitgeschichte.* I. *Das Judentum Palästinas zur Zeit Jesu und der Apostel.* Hamburg: Furche Verlag, third revised edition, 1959.

Describes the Jewish historical background to the New Testament beginning with the Babylonian exile, as well as the various sects of Judaism. Offers more detailed discussion of Pharisaism and its rabbinic tradition of second century A.D.

345 J. B. Frey (ed.). *Corpus Inscriptionum Judaicarum.* 2 vols. Rome: Institute of Christian Archaeology, 1936, 1952. Vol. 1 revised by B. Lifshitz: New York: Ktav, 1975.

Standard and important corpus. See no. 438 for a newer edition of the Egyptian materials.

346 L. L. Grabbe. *Judaism from Cyrus to Hadrian.* 2 vols. Minneapolis: Fortress, 1991/London: SCM, 1994.

Summaries of the major critical issues regarding Judaism in the hellenistic period, with bibliography. The summaries and bibliographies are generally reliable, although one cannot be equally expert in all areas. Grabbe is probably more critical of Hengel (no. 348) than one needs to be. Vol. 1 focuses on the Persian and Greek periods, Vol. 2 on the Roman period.

347 W. S. Green (ed.). *Approaches to Ancient Judaism II.* Brown Judaica Series. Chico: Scholars Press, 1980.

Included in this collection are timely essays regarding the use of Jewish materials in the study of the New Testament, including J. Neusner's "The Use of the Later Rabbinic Evidence for the Study of Paul" (pp. 4–63). Dated but worthwhile.

348 M. Hengel. *Judaism and Hellenism: Studies in their Encounter in Palestine during the Early Hellenistic Period.* 2 vols. Translated by J. Bowden. Philadelphia: Fortress/London: SCM, 1974. Original title: *Judentum und Hellenismus: Studien zu ihrer Begegnung unter besonderer Berücksichtigung Palästinas bis zur Mitte des 2 Jh.s v. Chr.* WUNT 10. Tübingen: Mohr-Siebeck, 1969. Second edition: 1973.

An excellent resource that shows the hellenistic influences on Palestinian and Diaspora Judaism in the time before and during the first century. Packed with valuable information and a standard reference. The footnotes in vol. 2 are a mine of information, often more valuable than the text in vol. 1.

349 M. Hengel. *The Zealots: Investigations into the Jewish Freedom Movement in the Period from Herod I until 70 A.D.*

Translated by D. Smith. Edinburgh: T. & T. Clark, 1989. Original title: *Die Zeloten: Untersuchungen zur Jüdischen Freiheitsbewegung in der Zeit von Herodes I. bis 70 n. Chr.* Leiden: Brill, 1961. Second edition: 1976.

Investigation of the various freedom movements in Palestine from the time of Herod the Great to the Fall of Jerusalem. Discusses the Jewish movement from the Maccabean struggles to Josephus documenting the Zealotic history in Palestine. This is the standard work on the subject.

350 R. A. Horsley with J. S. Hanson. *Bandits, Prophets, and Messiahs: Popular Movements at the Time of Jesus.* San Francisco: Harper & Row, 1985.

A study of the Jewish social context of early Christianity, including the religious sects of Palestine in the first century and before. Helpful section on the Zealots as well. Essential reading on this topic.

351 P. W. van der Horst. *Essays on the Jewish World of Early Christianity.* NTOA 14. Freiburg: Universitätsverlag/Göttingen: Vandenhoeck & Ruprecht, 1990.

Although these essays deal with various Jewish themes and writings, they are written with a focus on the context of the Greco-Roman world. Some are highly technical, but most are rewarding.

352 J. Jeremias. *Jerusalem in the Time of Jesus: An Investigation into Economic and Social Conditions during the New Testament Period.* Translated by F. H. Cave and C. H. Cave. Philadelphia: Fortress/London: SCM, 1969. Original title: *Jerusalem zur Zeit Jesu.* Göttingen: Vandenhoeck & Ruprecht, 1962.

Wealth of information, although many would comment that it is now out of date, certainly in approach. Worth consulting.

353 R. A. Kraft and G. W. E. Nickelsburg (eds.). *Early Judaism and its Modern Interpreters.* BMI. Atlanta: Scholars Press, 1986.

A "state of the art" type volume that selects prominent scholars to share not only what is happening in early Judaism and its literature, but also what is currently going on in the research. Helpful bibliographies are offered for each topic. A must for any interested in second temple and later Judaism. Caution: some sections are dated.

354 S. T. Lachs. *A Rabbinic Commentary on the New Testament: The Gospels of Matthew, Mark and Luke.* New Jersey: Ktav/New York: Anti-Defamation League of B'Nai B'Rith, 1987.

Rabbinic parallels are mustered in an attempt to elucidate the Gospels. Does it work? Occasionally. Some anachronistic reading of the second century into the first occurs.

355 A. R. C. Leaney. *The Jewish and Christian World: 200 B.C. to A.D. 200.* CC. Cambridge: Cambridge University Press, 1984.

Excellent background information on Judaism in the time before and contemporary with early Christianity. Contains special focus on Judaism outside of Palestine, origins of the synagogue, sects of Judaism, early rabbinic Judaism, and the history of the Jews from the time of the Seleucids. Its compact information and not well illustrated text, make it difficult for some students to digest. Overall it is balanced but somewhat dated.

356 J. Limburg (ed. and trans.). *Judaism: An Introduction for Christians.* Minneapolis: Augsburg, 1987.

Essays by informed scholars on the Jewish context of early Christianity that describe the Judaism from which early Christianity emerged and with which it was in dialogue. Also addresses the latent anti-Semitism in historic Christianity.

357 H. Maccoby. *Early Rabbinic Writings.* CC. Cambridge: Cambridge University Press, 1988.

A compact introduction to the rabbinic literature together with selections of that literature to illustrate certain characteristics. Valuable reference tool for students of this period.

358 H. Maccoby. *Judaism in the First Century.* Issues in Religious Studies. London: Sheldon, 1989.

A short introduction to the "major players" in Judaism in the first century, along with the major religious rituals. Such an approach has been challenged by E. P. Sanders (see no. 378).

359 J. S. McLaren. *Power and Politics in Palestine: The Jews and the Governing of their Land 100 b.c.–a.d. 70.* JSNTSup 63. Sheffield: JSOT Press, 1991.

Inspired and supervised by E. P. Sanders, this study emphasizes the role of the laity and "chief priests" in the administration of Palestine, rejecting the notion of the Jews being separatists and noting their cooperation with the Romans, rendering the war of a.d. 66–70 not inevitable.

360 M. McNamara. *Palestinian Judaism and the New Testament.* GNS 4. Wilmington, Del.: Michael Glazier, 1983.

A balanced guide to the Judaisms from the first centuries b.c. and a.d. and to the rabbinic Judaism of the second to the fourth century. An excellent introduction to the literature emanating from Palestine in relation to understanding the Jewish people and the New Testament. McNamara does an especially good job with the lesser known materials, with which he is closely familiar, such as the Targum.

361 M. McNamara. *Targum and Testament: Aramaic Paraphrases of the Hebrew Bible—A Light on the New Testament.* Grand Rapids: Eerdmans/Shannon: Irish University Press, 1972.

A standard and extremely helpful guide to the Targums, including discussion of their relevance for the New Testament and an exposition of the Targums themselves.

362 C. G. Montefiore and H. Loewe (eds.). *A Rabbinic Anthology.* London: Macmillan, 1938. Reprinted Cleveland: Meridian and Jewish Publication Society of America, 1963/New York: Schocken, 1974.

A handy collection of rabbinic material, gathered, classified, and translated by the editors. One must be cautious regarding use of this material, however. Some of the rabbinic sources are much too late to be of any use in understanding the New Testament, while even the earliest have to be manipulated in order to have application before A.D. 70. The reference system is not always the standard one used.

363 G. F. Moore. *Judaism in the First Centuries of the Christian Era: The Age of the Tannaim.* 3 vols. Cambridge: Harvard University Press, 1927–30.

A proven though now dated analysis.

364 M. J. Mulder (ed.). *Mikra: Text, Translation, Reading and Interpretation of the Hebrew Bible in Ancient Judaism and Early Christianity.* CRINT. Assen/Maastricht: Van Gorcum/Minneapolis: Fortress, 1990.

A hefty volume by Jewish and Christian scholars who try to explain the world of Judaism and early Christianity. The collection of essays is by prominent scholars who generally argue their cases well, but not always. Fairly well documented.

365 J. Neusner. *Introduction to Rabbinic Literature.* ABRL. Garden City: Doubleday, 1994.

A sizable volume for the beginning student, but also one that will enable the advanced student to learn about Judaism in antiquity, including the various sects of Judaism in the first century. There are generous selections of primary texts that illustrate the author's points. Carefully gives the historical context and significance of the Mishnah, Tosephta, Talmudim, and Sifre as well as the various midrashim on biblical texts.

366 J. Neusner. *Judaism in the Beginning of Christianity.* Philadelphia: Fortress/London: SPCK, 1984.

A useful summary by an acknowledged master of the subject. The various chapters are excerpted from various others of Neusner's many writings. Especially helpful on Hillel, the Pharisees, and the destruction of the temple and its effect on Judaism.

367 J. Neusner. *Judaism and Christianity in the Age of Constantine: History, Messiah, Israel, and the Initial Confrontation.* Chicago/London: University of Chicago Press, 1987.

Written by a master in the field who explains in part that the Judaism that prevailed at a later time in Israel was not the one that prevailed in the first century as Christianity emerged. Helpful information on Talmudic Judaism with comparisons and contrasts with Christianity. Helpful discussion of formation of the Jewish and Christian biblical canons.

368 J. Neusner. *Judaism: The Evidence of the Mishnah.* Chicago: University of Chicago Press, 1981.
An important but controversial work. Not all agree with Neusner's methods or conclusions, but neither are they easy to dismiss.

369 J. Neusner. *Judaism in the Matrix of Christianity.* Philadelphia: Fortress, 1986.
Focuses on the "outsider," the city, the Messiah, and Torah and its meaning as understood by first- and second-century Judaism. Claims that Judaism emerged in response to the crisis brought on by the triumph of Christianity. Arguments are critical, cogent, and require a response.

370 J. Neusner. *Midrash in Context: Exegesis in Formative Judaism.* The Foundations of Judaism: Method, Teleology, Doctrine. Part One. Philadelphia: Fortress, 1983.
Treats the Judaism that obtained following the destruction of the temple with special focus on the understanding of revelation, scripture, and canon in Judaism. Has useful collection of ancient exegeses and a bibliography on Midrash at the end.

371 J. Neusner, P. Borgen, E. S. Frerichs, and R. Horsley (eds.). *The Social World of Formative Christianity and Judaism.* (H. C. Kee Festschrift). Philadelphia: Fortress, 1988.
A festschrift for H. C. Kee that has an impressive list of international scholars offering some nineteen essays on ancient Judaism at the emergence of early Christianity.

372 G. W. E. Nickelsburg. *Jewish Literature between the Bible and the Mishnah: A Historical and Literary Introduction.* Philadelphia: Fortress, 1981.
An introduction to the context and corpus of the apocrypha and pseudepigrapha. Well organized and numerous examples from the primary sources.

373 D. Patte. *Early Jewish Hermeneutic in Palestine.* SBLDS 22. Missoula: Scholars Press, 1975.

> A useful treatment of Jewish hermeneutics: That is, the ways in which the Jews interpreted their Scriptures.

374 H. G. Perelmuter. *Siblings: Rabbinic Judaism and Early Christianity at their Beginnings.* New York: Paulist, 1989.

> Shows how both rabbinic Judaism and early Christianity emerged from the same "stream of development" and how each was motivated by messianic consciousness and a desire for covenant survival. Rabbinic sources are cited in abundance throughout.

375 A. J. Saldarini. *Pharisees, Scribes and Sadducees in Palestinian Society: A Sociological Approach.* Wilmington, Del.: Michael Glazier, 1988.

> A responsible text on the sects of Judaism in the time of the New Testament, but also more broadly from 200 B.C. to A.D. 200. Saldarini surveys these groups from the perspectives of Josephus, the New Testament, and rabbinic Judaism.

376 E. P. Sanders (ed.). *Jewish and Christian Self-Definition.* I. *The Shaping of Christianity in the Second and Third Centuries.* II. Edited with A. I. Baumgarten and A. Mendelson. *Aspects of Judaism in the Graeco-Roman Period.* Philadelphia: Fortress/London: SCM, 1980, 1981.

> Valuable collections of essays by prominent scholars who focus on the Jewish milieu of early Christianity as well as its encounter with gnosticism.

377 E. P. Sanders. *Jewish Law from Jesus to the Mishnah: Five Studies.* Philadelphia: Trinity Press International/London: SCM, 1990.

> Five important studies on Jewish law, further establishing his position in distinction to others such as J. Neusner.

378 E. P. Sanders. *Judaism: Practice and Belief 63 B.C.E.–66 C.E.* Philadelphia: Trinity Press International/London: SCM, 1992.

> A massive but enjoyable book on the Jewish people and their various religious practices and beliefs. Sanders attempts to get away from stereotyping Judaism on the

basis of the Pharisees, etc., and to look at the ongoing debate of the time.

379 E. P. Sanders. *Paul and Palestinian Judaism: A Comparison of Patterns of Religion.* Philadelphia: Fortress/London: SCM, 1977.

This is the book that marks the turning point in the new perspective on Paul, although most of it is devoted to a study of Palestinian Judaism from Sanders's perspective. The field is divided among those who accept and reject his analysis with respect to both Judaism and Paul.

380 E. Schürer. *A History of the Jewish People in the Time of Jesus Christ.* Translated by J. Macpherson, S. Taylor, and P. Christie. 6 vols. Edinburgh: T. & T. Clark, 1885–91. *The History of the Jewish People in the Age of Jesus Christ (175 B.C.–A.D. 135).* Translated, revised, and edited by G. Vermes, F. Millar, M. Goodman, and M. Black. 3 vols. Edinburgh: T. & T. Clark, 1973–87. Original title: *Geschichte des jüdischen Volkes im Zeitalter Jesu Christi.* 2 vols. Leipzig: second edition, 1886–90 [third edition 1898–1902, fourth edition 1907–11]), second edition of *Lehrbuch der neutestamentlichen Zeitgeschichte.* Leipzig: 1874.

Describes the history and social context of Judaism from the years 175 B.C. to A.D. 135. The classic text on the subject, though is now dated in some sections. The references to primary sources are still quite valuable, however, for any study of this period.

381 R. M. Seltzer (ed.). *Judaism: A People and its History.* Religion, History, and Culture Selections from *The Encyclopedia of Religion.* Edited by M. Eliade. New York: Macmillan, 1987, 1989.

Parts I and II are valuable discussions of the Jewish religion and the Judaism that was contemporary with the emergence of early Christianity.

382 H. Shanks (ed.). *Christianity and Rabbinic Judaism: A Parallel History of their Origins and Early Development.* Washington, D.C.: Biblical Archaeology Society, 1992/London: SPCK, 1993.

Essays by Jewish and Christian scholars on the origins and development of both Judaism and early Christianity and where they interlock at various junctures. Useful and informed.

383 H. D. Slingerland. *The Testaments of the Twelve Patriarchs: A Critical History of Research.* Missoula: Scholars Press, 1975.

Much has happened since, but this provides a useful guide.

384 A. Sperber (ed.). *The Bible in Aramaic.* 4 vols. Leiden: Brill, 1959–68.

The standard text.

385 H. L. Strack and P. Billerbeck, with J. Jeremias. *Kommentar zum Neuen Testament aus Talmud und Midrasch.* 6 vols. Munich: Beck, 1922–61.

Although frequently criticized for method and approach, Strack-Billerbeck still provides a significant compendium of rabbinic texts, if rightly used.

386 H. L. Strack and G. Stemberger. *Introduction to the Talmud and Midrash.* Translated by M. Bockmuel. Minneapolis: Fortress/Edinburgh: T. & T. Clark, 1992. Original title: *Einleitung in Talmud und Midrasch.* Munich: Beck, 1982.

Carefully written introduction that the scholars in the field could read with advantage. Cites numerous examples from the Talmudic literature and useful discussion of Midrashim. The careful reader will find some parallels here with the way early Christianity interpreted its Scriptures.

387 S. Talmon (ed.). *Jewish Civilization in the Hellenistic Roman Period.* Philadelphia: Trinity Press International, 1991.

Discusses Jewish literature from the pre-Christian era to the second century A.D. Includes articles on history, society, and literature, as well as a careful look at the parallels between the Qumran literature and rabbinic Judaism and early Christianity.

388 V. A. Tcherikover and A. Fuks (eds.). *Corpus Papyrorum Judaicarum*. 3 vols. Cambridge: Harvard University Press, 1957–64.

> A standard collection of Jewish papyri sources, still worth consulting.

389 G. Vermes and M. D. Goodman (eds.). *The Essenes according to the Classical Sources*. Sheffield: JSOT Press, 1989.

> The major sources cited in Greek and facing-page translation by Philo, Pliny, Josephus, Dio, Hegesippus, and Hippolytus of Rome.

390 M. Whittaker. *Jews and Christians: Greco-Roman Views.* CC. Cambridge: Cambridge University Press, 1984.

> An important introduction and anthology of texts related to how others saw the Jews and Christians of antiquity. Valuable section on Jewish religious practices as well as an examination of the main strands of paganism that both the Jews and Christians encountered in the Greco-Roman world.

12.2 Qumran Studies: The Dead Sea Scrolls

Along with the volumes that are listed below, a recent journal, *Dead Sea Discoveries: A Journal of Current Research on the Scrolls and Related Literature*, will be of special interest to the student of Qumran studies. With the recent release of the scrolls from scholarly captivity, there has been the inevitable flood of publications of both texts and analyses. Consequently, the relevance of the scrolls for understanding the New Testament has once more come to the fore as an issue of popular and scholarly debate. The following volumes are not exhaustive, but representative of the standard works in the field.

391 D. Barthélemy and J. T. Milik et al. (eds.). *Discoveries in the Judaean Desert*. Oxford: Clarendon, 1955–.

> Thirteen volumes of primary texts with translations and notes have been produced to date, the most recent appearing in 1994. Excellent resources.

392 J. H. Charlesworth (ed.). *The Dead Sea Scrolls: Hebrew, Aramaic, and Greek Texts with English Translations*. Louisville: Westminster/John Knox/Tübingen: Mohr-Siebeck, 1993– .

> Promises to be the complete set of texts.

393 J. H. Charlesworth (ed.). *Jesus and the Dead Sea Scrolls.* ABRL. New York: Doubleday, 1992.

> A collection of essays by prominent biblical scholars who observe the similarities and differences between Jesus and the Dead Sea scrolls, but especially their value in helping to know more about the times in which Jesus lived.

394 J. H. Charlesworth (ed.). *John and Qumran.* London: Geoffrey Chapman, 1972. Second edition: *John and the Dead Sea Scrolls.* New York: Crossroad, 1990.

> These essays raise the intriguing question of the parallels between John's Gospel and the Dead Sea scrolls. An older treatment that has been revised and added to (Chapters 1 and 5) and made more relevant. Important in placing the origins of the Gospel of John in a Jewish setting.

395 F. M. Cross, Jr. *The Ancient Library of Qumran and Modern Biblical Studies.* Garden City, N.Y.: Doubleday, 1958. Second edition: 1961. Reprint edition: Sheffield: JSOT Press, 1994.

> A classic text by one of the prominent researchers involved in the translating and editing of the scrolls. Shows how the scrolls bring clarity to a number of biblical texts.

396 R. Eisenman and M. Wise. *The Dead Sea Scrolls Uncovered: The First Complete Translation and Interpretation of 50 Key Documents withheld for over 35 Years.* Shaftesbury, England: Element Books, 1992.

> Sensational as the title suggests, but an important step in the release of the scrolls that had been kept from public domain for so long. The value and accuracy of the translations are disputed by a number of scholars. Translations of several important texts, including 4QMMT.

397 J. A. Fitzmyer. *The Dead Sea Scrolls: Major Publications and Tools for Study.* SBLRBS 20. Atlanta: Scholars Press, 1975. Second edition: 1990.

> Authoritative reference tool.

398 F. G. Martinez. *The Dead Sea Scrolls Translated: The Qumran Texts in English.* Leiden: Brill, 1994.

> The most comprehensive and authoritative translation available. Includes newly released documents in very readable form. A must.

399 J. Murphy-O'Connor (ed.). *Paul and Qumran: Studies in New Testament Exegesis.* Chicago: Priory, 1968. Second edition: *Paul and the Dead Sea Scrolls.* New York: Crossroad, 1990.

> Carefully written essays on the interpretation of Paul's writings in light of the Dead Sea scrolls. Several interesting parallels are observed and shown to be relevant in exegeting Paul. Does not tie Paul to Qumran, but to elements of Judaism common to both.

400 H. Shanks, J. Vanderkam, P. K. McCarter, Jr., and J. A. Sanders. *The Dead Sea Scrolls after Forty Years.* Washington, D.C.: Biblical Archaeology Society, 1991.

> A small book that explains the significance of the scrolls for biblical studies and their relation to biblical faith, both Jewish and Christian. McCarter's essay is especially relevant for understanding the Judaistic context of early Christianity. Written for the lay person.

401 H. Shanks (ed.). *Understanding the Dead Sea Scrolls: A Reader from the Biblical Archaeology Review.* New York: Random House, 1992.

> A collection of essays by scrolls experts who provide a careful introduction to the discovery and significance of the scrolls. The topics covered include the origins of the sect at Qumran, a discussion of the Temple Scroll, how the scrolls are similar to and different from early Christianity and later rabbinic Judaism, the Copper Scroll, the Vatican's role in keeping the scrolls from publication (a not too convincing argument), and an interview of sorts with John Strugnell, former chief editor of the scrolls. Most of the sections are worth reading, but not all are illuminating.

402 K. Stendahl (ed.). *The Scrolls and the New Testament.* New York: Crossroad, 1957.

This is one of the classic texts that scholars appeal to when focusing on the significance of the Dead Sea scrolls for study of the New Testament. Although old, these essays still deserve attentive reading.

403 G. Vermes. *The Dead Sea Scrolls: Qumran in Perspective.* London: Collins, 1977. Third edition: London: SCM, 1994.
Very useful text on the background and significance of the scrolls by a competent scrolls scholar.

404 G. Vermes. *The Dead Sea Scrolls in English.* Harmondsworth: Penguin, 1962. Third edition: Harmondsworth: Penguin/Sheffield: JSOT Press, 1987.
Perhaps the most useful standard translation.

405 M. O. Wise, N. Golb, J. J. Collins, and D. G. Pardee (eds.). *Methods of Investigation of the Dead Sea Scrolls and the Khirbet Qumran Site: Present Realities and Future Prospects.* Annals of the New York Academy of Sciences 722. New York: New York Academy of Sciences, 1994.
A collection of twenty-six papers on the history of the Qumran site, studies of the texts and methodologies employed for interpreting them, the origins of the scrolls themselves, and the role the scrolls played in formative Judaism. An impressive collection of who's who Qumran scholars who frequently disagree dramatically on the significance and meaning of these documents.

12.3 Jewish Apocalyptic

Much work has been done in this area recently. The traditional definition of apocalyptic has emphasized the literary and theological dimensions. The analysis of apocalyptic that resulted was based on seeing whether a given text exemplified the requisite number of features, such as a heavenly vision or a certain kind of eschatology. In more recent times the analysis of apocalyptic has been determined upon a grid or matrix that attempts to plot a text's location in terms of various sociological features as well. There have been some objections to this view, but it seems to have established itself as the consensus.

406 J. J. Collins (ed.). *Apocalypse: The Morphology of a Genre. Semeia* 14. Chico: Scholars Press, 1979.

The definition of apocalyptic according to the matrix approach that came about through years of discussion at the Society of Biblical Literature meetings. There are various contributors, but Collins's summary statement is probably the most important.

407 J. J. Collins. *The Apocalyptic Imagination: An Introduction to the Jewish Matrix of Christianity.* New York: Crossroad, 1984.

Reflects the matrix approach toward apocalyptic, which attempts to define the concept through sociological, theological, and literary criteria. Collins includes useful analyses of the range of apocalyptic literature, providing some very helpful proposals for interpretation of such troublesome books as Daniel.

408 J. J. Collins and J. H. Charlesworth (eds.). *Mysteries and Revelations: Apocalyptic Studies since the Uppsala Colloquium.* JSPSup 9. Sheffield: JSOT Press, 1991.

Essays that continue the discussion begun in Uppsala (see no. 410). Particularly useful are contributions by D. Hellholm and J. J. Collins.

409 P. D. Hanson (ed.). *Visionaries and their Apocalypses.* Issues in Religion and Theology 2. Philadelphia: Fortress/London: SPCK, 1983.

A fine representative collection of essays on apocalyptic, including those by K. Koch, P. D. Hanson, J. J. Collins, M. Stone, J. Z. Smith, N. Perrin, and J. G. Gager. Many of these represent some of the influential writers in the field over the course of the last forty years.

410 D. Hellholm (ed.). *Apocalypticism in the Mediterranean World and the Near East.* Tübingen: Mohr-Siebeck, 1983.

A large, extensive, and very important work on apocalyptic, the results of a conference in Uppsala. Contributors to the debate include Hellholm, E. P. Sanders, M. Smith, W. Meeks, J. J. Collins, among many others. Contributions are in English, German, and French.

411 E. Käsemann. "The Beginnings of Christian Theology." Pp. 82–107 in *New Testament Questions of Today.* Translated by W. J. Montague. Philadelphia: Fortress/London: SCM,

1969. Original title: *Exegetische Versuche und Besinnungen*. Vol. 2. Göttingen: Vandenhoeck & Ruprecht, 1965.

A very important essay that helped to revive discussion of apocalyptic, setting an agenda that has proved influential. Käsemann argues that apocalyptic was the mother of Christianity. Many have disputed this.

412 K. Koch. *The Rediscovery of Apocalyptic: A Polemical Work on a Neglected Area of Biblical Studies and its Damaging Effects on Theology and Philosophy.* SBT 2/22. Translated by M. Kohl. Nashville: Allenson/London: SCM, 1972. Original title: *Ratlos vor der Apokalyptik*. Gütersloh: Mohn, 1970.

Part of the (apparently successful) attempt to revive interest in apocalyptic, giving it its due in relation to prophecy as a useful category for understanding the emergence of Christianity.

413 L. Morris. *Apocalyptic*. Grand Rapids: Eerdmans, 1972.

A solid exposition of the older school of thought on apocalyptic, which defined it according to a number of literary and theological features. Useful as a very basic introduction.

414 C. Rowland. *The Open Heaven: A Study of Apocalyptic in Judaism and in Early Christianity*. London: SPCK, 1982.

A major revision to the current definitions of apocalyptic, seeing the vision of heaven rather than eschatology as predominant. Important study, even if reductionistic and not ultimately convincing. Rowland's apocalyptic orientation influences his views of the origins of Christianity (see no. 685).

415 D. S. Russell. *The Method and Message of Jewish Apocalyptic 200 B.C.–A.D. 100*. Philadelphia: Westminster/London: SCM, 1964.

The standard treatment of apocalyptic from the standpoint of categorization by major literary and theological features.

12.4 Jewish Interpretation/Midrash and the Use of the Old Testament in the New

416 J. W. Aageson. *Written Also for Our Sake: Paul and the Art of Biblical Interpretation.* Louisville: Westminster/John Knox, 1993.

Aageson uses what he calls a conversation model of hermeneutics, one that is not restricted to literary or critical concerns but attempts to find a way that shows the continuing relevance of Scripture.

417 G. Archer and G. Chirichigno. *Old Testament Quotations in the New Testament: A Complete Survey.* Chicago: Moody, 1983.

Despite the oddity of the subtitle this is a brief presentation in Hebrew and Greek of the Old Testament quotations in the New Testament, with notes on their relationships. The texts are useful to have even if the explanations are not always convincing. Theological concerns interfere with some conclusions.

418 D. L. Baker. *Two Testaments, One Bible: A Study of the Theological Relationship between the Old and New Testaments.* Downers Grove/Leicester: InterVarsity, 1976. Second edition: 1991.

A detailed study of the use of the Old Testament in the New. Particularly useful is the section on typology.

419 D. A. Carson and H. G. M. Williamson (eds.). *It is Written: Scripture Citing Scripture—Essays in Honour of B. Lindars.* Cambridge: Cambridge University Press, 1988.

Each author or corpus is analyzed by someone supposed to be expert in the area. Several of the essays are insightful, such as Carson's on John, but others lack specificity. Contributors include I. H. Marshall, M. Hooker, M. Smith, R. Bauckham, and G. Beale.

420 B. D. Chilton. *A Galilean Rabbi and his Bible: Jesus' Use of the Interpreted Scripture of his Time.* GNS 8. Wilmington, Del.: Michael Glazier, 1984. British edition: *A Galilean Rabbi and his Bible: Jesus' Own Interpretation of Isaiah.* London: SPCK, 1984.

Illustrates the importance of Targumic research for understanding the New Testament, especially the teaching of Jesus. Brief but competent.

421 E. E. Ellis. *Paul's Use of the Old Testament.* Edinburgh/London: Oliver & Boyd, 1957. Reprinted Grand Rapids: Baker, 1981.

Ellis sees Paul as a grammatical-historical interpreter of the Old Testament, using the texts in an extended though legitimate way. He has continued to develop this idea in several subsequent works.

422 C. A. Evans and J. A. Sanders (eds.). *Paul and the Scriptures of Israel.* JSNTSup 83. SSEJC 1. Sheffield: JSOT Press, 1993.

In two parts, the first includes responses to Hays's *Echoes of Scripture* (see no. 426), and the second has a number of essays on the topic of the use of the Old Testament in the New, several of which are methodologically insightful, including those by C. Stanley and J. Scott.

423 C. A. Evans and W. R. Stegner (eds.). *The Gospel and the Scriptures of Israel.* JSNTSup 104. SSEJC 3. Sheffield: JSOT Press, 1994.

Essays in five parts—John and Jesus, Matthew, Mark, Luke, and John. A range of contributors and many significant and insightful essays.

424 R. T. France. *Jesus and the Old Testament.* Downers Grove: InterVarsity/London: Tyndale, 1971.

An older work, but still of use.

425 L. Goppelt. *Typos: The Typological Interpretation of the Old Testament in the New.* Translated by J. E. Alsup. Grand Rapids: Eerdmans, 1982. Original title: *Typos: Die typologische Deutung des Alten Testaments im Neuen.* Darmstadt: Wissenschaftliche, 1966.

One of few studies to take the concept of typology seriously. For Goppelt it becomes a broad interpretive tool to understand the relationship between the Testaments. Important contribution.

426 R. B. Hays. *Echoes of Scripture in the Letters of Paul.* New Haven/London: Yale University Press, 1989.

In this highly influential study of the use of the Old Testament in Paul, Hays develops the idea of intertextuality (although not in quite the same way as literary critics would) to explore Paul's ecclesiocentric rather than Christocentric hermeneutics (see no. 422, where Hays defends and modifies his views).

427 D. Juel. *Messianic Exegesis: Christological Interpretation of the Old Testament in Early Christianity.* Philadelphia: Fortress, 1988.

Emphasis upon and analysis of the concept of messianic exegesis.

428 B. Lindars. *New Testament Apologetic: The Doctrinal Significance of the Old Testament Quotations.* London: SCM, 1961.

Lindars develops the idea that the Old Testament served as a kind of "testimony" document that was applied and modified by the New Testament writers.

429 R. Longenecker. *Biblical Exegesis in the Apostolic Period.* Grand Rapids: Eerdmans, 1975.

Describes the diversity of exegesis present in the first century on the basis of various Jewish models available, and then sees how these are illustrated in the biblical writers. He concludes that while some of this is applicable today, much of this exegesis apparently is not valid now.

430 B. G. Schuchard. *Scripture within Scripture: The Interrelationship of Form and Function in the Explicit Old Testament Citations in the Gospel of John.* SBLDS 133. Atlanta: Scholars Press, 1992.

Not the best treatment (since he fails to deal with the question of function, and virtually always opts for the Septuagint form), but the most recent, with helpful bibliography.

431 C. D. Stanley. *Paul and the Language of Scripture: Citation Technique in the Pauline Epistles and Contemporary Literature.* SNTSMS 74. Cambridge: Cambridge University Press, 1992.

An analysis of Paul's use of the Old Testament, in particular the Septuagint, in terms of his similarities to and differences from the use of authoritative writings in the ancient world. Paul ends up standing between a rigid formalism and a very stylized use. It is good to see Paul's Greek background properly explored.

13

Greco-Roman World

The Greco-Roman world was a highly complex one, and made more difficult for study by New Testament scholars for several reasons. First is the tendency, at least within the last fifty years or so, to emphasize Jewish backgrounds. A corrective to this has begun within the last ten to twenty years, as it has been increasingly recognized that whatever the distinctives of Judaism the Jewish people were only one ethnic group among many living within the larger scope of the Greco-Roman world. Secondly, the Greco-Roman world itself is a difficult phenomenon to describe. To speak simplistically, on the one hand it continued many of the cultural, linguistic, and artistic institutions of the Alexandrian (and thus earlier Greek) hegemony, established in the fourth century B.C. as the result of the far-reaching conquests of Alexander the Great. On the other hand the Romans brought many of their own distinctives with regard to the organization and institutionalization of religion, government, and economics. Rome itself had recently undergone the transition from republic to empire, and the New Testament world benefited from the results of a strong central authority. Thirdly, Palestine was not at the center of anybody's interests (apart possibly from those of Palestinians themselves). Thus in studying the world of the New Testament one is studying something on the outskirts of the empire. This does not mean that the empire did not extend its control and in-

fluence this far, but does mean that in some ways it is more difficult to identify the ways in which the empire influenced Palestinian life than it would be to investigate, for instance, Rome.
Fourthly, there is much diversity even within Palestine. For example, it is being recognized that life in Galilee was different in
many respects from life in Jerusalem. So generalizations may
only have limited application. Fifthly, there is the limitation of
the evidence. Most of the papyri—so useful for linguistic study—
come from Egypt, although there are a few significant resources
from the eastern Mediterranean and elsewhere. There are inscriptions, but there is always the question of how indicative and representative they are. Literary figures such as Josephus write from
distinct perspectives that must be taken into account—they are
hardly objective. The literary remains of many of the writers of
the hellenistic world never survived, since emphasis was placed
upon the "classical" authors. This makes it extremely difficult to
reconstruct what life was like in the Greco-Roman world of Palestine. However, in many ways researchers are fortunate because,
despite the limitations, there is probably more evidence for the
ancient Greek and Roman worlds than any other ancient civilization. But the evidence requires careful interpretation. The published primary and secondary sources are numerous. Below is a
list of some of the more important ones with reference to the
New Testament. See F. W. Danker. *A Century of Greco-Roman
Philology: Featuring the American Philological Association and
the Society of Biblical Literature*. Atlanta: Scholars Press, 1988,
for discussion and bibliography.

13.1 Primary Sources

See under epistolary form for more primary sources, in particular papyri letters.

13.1.1 Anthologies and Handbooks

432 C. K. Barrett. *The New Testament Background: Selected
Documents*. London: SPCK, 1956/New York: Harper, 1961.
Second edition: 1987.
   Probably the best collection of its kind. All in translation.

433 D. L. Dungan and D. R. Cartlidge. *Sourcebook of Texts for
the Comparative Study of the Gospels*. Missoula: Scholars

Press, 1973. Revised edition: *Documents for the Study of the Gospels*. Philadelphia: Fortress/London: Collins, 1980.

A number of texts focused upon the Gospels. All in translation.

434 H. C. Kee. *The Origins of Christianity: Sources and Documents*. Englewood Cliffs: Prentice-Hall/London: SPCK, 1973. Second edition: 1980.

Useful but not as much as Barrett offers. All in translation.

13.1.2 Epigraphy

There are many other resources available in the area of papyri, inscriptions, and ostraca. The sources below not only provide sufficient material for New Testament study but provide access to other sources. Still a useful volume is A. Deissmann's *Light from the Ancient East* (no. 475).

435 H. D. Betz (ed.). *The Greek Magical Papyri in Translation, including the Demotic Spells*. Chicago: University of Chicago Press, 1986.

This is a translation of the texts in K. Preisendanz (ed.). *Papyri Graecae Magicae: Die Griechischen Zauberpapyri*. 3 vols. Leipzig/Berlin: Teubner, 1928–42. Reprint edited by A. Heinrichs: Stuttgart: Teubner, 1973–77.

436 B. Grenfell et al. (eds.). *The Oxyrhynchus Papyri*. London: Egypt Exploration Society, 1889–.

The sixtieth volume of this series has now been reached, with more to come. The volumes vary in content, but nonliterary, literary, and biblical texts are all represented. The most significant texts published, so far as New Testament study is concerned, may well be the fragments of unknown Gospels (e.g., nos. 1, 654, 655, 840, 1081, 1224). See also H. I. Bell and T. C. Skeat (eds.). *Fragments of an Unknown Gospel and Other Early Christian Papyri*. London: British Museum, 1935. This text is known as P. Egerton 2, and it contains several large fragments of an unknown Gospel. There are many other papyri collections also worth looking at occasionally. They can be found through J. F. Oates et al. *Checklist of Editions of Greek Papyri and Ostraca*. Atlanta: American Society of Papyrologists, 1985.

437 P. W. van der Horst. *Ancient Jewish Epitaphs: An Introductory Survey of a Millennium of Jewish Funerary Epigraphy* (300 BCE–700 CE). CBET 2. Kampen: Kok Pharos, 1991.

This volume not only provides evidence for the widespread use of Greek among Palestinian Jews, as evidenced by their funerary inscriptions, but has an insightful chapter on the implications for study of the New Testament (pp. 127–43). Many original texts are given and translated.

438 W. Horbury and D. Noy (eds.). *Jewish Inscriptions of Graeco-Roman Egypt*. Cambridge: Cambridge University Press, 1992.

A fine collection of the Jewish inscriptions found in Egypt dating from the third century B.C. to the sixth century A.D. Each text is edited with a translation and notes. This is essentially the Egyptian section of Frey's *CIJ* (see no. 345), but with additions and further corrections.

439 G. H. R. Horsley et al. (eds.). *New Documents Illustrating Early Christianity*. 6 vols. to date. North Ryde, N. S. W., Australia: Ancient History Documentary Research Centre, Macquarie University, 1981–.

Volumes 1–4 and 6–7 (with others to follow) are anthologies of recently published papyri and inscriptions of relevance for study of the New Testament. Much of this material is being amassed to aid in a project to develop a new lexicon of hellenistic popular literature.

440 N. Lewis (ed.). *The Documents from the Bar Kokhba Period in the Cave of Letters: Greek Papyri.* Jerusalem: Israel Exploration Society, 1989.

A number of Greek letters from early in the second century in Palestine that illustrate the widespread use of Greek among Jews.

13.1.3 Literary Authors (may also include Epigraphy)

13.1.3.1 GREEK AND LATIN TEXTS (WITH OR WITHOUT TRANSLATION)

441 R. F. Hock and E. N. O'Neil (eds.). *The Chreia in Ancient Rhetoric*. I. *The Progymnasmata*. Atlanta: Scholars Press, 1986.

Texts regarding the theory and practice of chreia production with facing page translation and notes.

442 C. R. Holladay. *Fragments from Hellenistic Jewish Authors.* 2 vols. Chico: Scholars Press, 1983, 1989.

A valuable guide to primary sources, with facing page translations, as well as annotations.

443 A. A. Long and D. N. Sedley (eds.). *The Hellenistic Philosophers.* 2 vols. Cambridge: Cambridge University Press, 1977.

An excellent resource of primary texts from the range of hellenistic philosophers, with translations and annotations.

444 Loeb Classical Library. Cambridge: Harvard University Press/London: Heinemann.

These editions provide Greek or Latin text with facing page translation. This is the largest collection of ancient authors available. Whereas some of the texts are relatively old and in need of replacement for reasons of textual criticism or quality of translation, many are still the standard editions and virtually all are of value. The following are some of the most important authors for biblical studies.

Greek authors (including later Greek church authors): Achilles Tatius, Aeschylus (2 vols.), Apollodorus (2 vols.), Apollonius Rhodius, Appian (4 vols.), Aristophanes (3 vols.), Aristotle (23 vols.), Arrian (2 vols.), Basil (4 vols.), Clement of Alexandria, Demosthenes (7 vols.), Dio Cassius (9 vols.), Dio Chrysostom (5 vols.), Diodorus Siculus (12 vols.), Diogenes Laertius (2 vols.), Dionysius of Halicarnassus (9 vols.), Epictetus (2 vols.), Euripides (4 vols.), Eusebius (2 vols.), Greek Anthology (5 vols.), Herodotus (4 vols.), Hesiod, Hippocrates (6 vols.), Homer (4 vols.), Isocrates (3 vols.), Josephus (10 vols.), Lucian (8 vols.), Marcus Aurelius, Pausanias (5 vols.), Philo (12 vols.), Philostratus (2 vols.), Plato (12 vols.), Plotinus (7 vols.), Plutarch (26 vols. Lives and Moralia), Polybius (6 vols.), Procopius (7 vols.), Sextus Empiricus (4 vols.), Sophocles (2 vols.), Strabo (8 vols.), Thucydides (4 vols.), Xenophon

(7 vols.). Latin authors (including Latin church authors): Apuleius (2 vols.), Augustine (10 vols.), Bede (2 vols.), Caesar (3 vols.), Celsus (3 vols.), Cicero (28 vols.), Horace (2 vols.), Jerome, Livy (14 vols.), Ovid (6 vols.), Pliny (10 vols.), Pliny the Younger (2 vols.), Quintilian (4 vols.), Sallust, Seneca (10 vols.), Seneca the Elder (2 vols.), Suetonius (2 vols.), Tacitus (5 vols.), Varro (2 vols.), Virgil (2 vols.).

445 A. J. Malherbe (ed.). *The Cynic Epistles.* SBLSBS 12. Atlanta: Scholars Press, 1977.

The Cynic epistles in Greek with translation. The influence of cynicism has probably been grossly overestimated in New Testament study.

446 M. Stern (ed.). *Greek and Latin Authors on Jews and Judaism.* 3 vols. Jerusalem: Israel Academy of Sciences and Humanities, 1974–84.

A valuable collection of primary and secondary sources illustrating thought in the ancient Greco-Roman world. The format allows the reader to establish the significance of the selections.

447 Texts and Translations Series, Graeco-Roman Religions Series. Atlanta: Scholars Press.

Many important and lesser known authors are included, not all of equal value. Important for study of the New Testament are *Teles* and Pseudo-Lucian's *De Dea Syria,* among others.

13.1.3.2 ENGLISH TRANSLATIONS

448 M. M. Austin (ed.). *The Hellenistic World from Alexander to the Roman Conquest: A Selection of Ancient Sources in Translation.* Cambridge: Cambridge University Press, 1981.

Probably the best collection of primary sources in translation concerning the hellenistic world. Although the period covered ended before the advent of Christianity, early Christianity grew up in a world created for the most part by the results chronicled in these selections.

449 R. S. Bagnall and P. Derow. *Greek Historical Documents: The Hellenistic Period.* Chico: Scholars Press, 1981.

Excellent collection of translated sources reflecting the historical context in which Christianity developed.

450 J. R. Bartlett. *Jews in the Hellenistic World: Josephus, Aristeas, the Sibylline Oracles, Eupolemus.* CC. Cambridge: Cambridge University Press, 1985.

Basic collection conveniently presented with important comments.

451 B. P. Copenhaver. *Hermetica: The Greek Corpus Hermeticum and the Latin Asclepius in a New English Translation, with Notes and Introduction.* Cambridge: Cambridge University Press, 1992.

A clear and useful English translation based upon the French Budé edition (A. D. Nock and A. J. Festugière [eds.]. *Corpus Hermeticum.* 4 vols. Paris: Belles Lettres, 1954–60), the best critical edition available. Earlier English translations, including W. Scott's (4 vols. Oxford: Clarendon, 1924–36), are unreliable because of their precritical texts.

452 R. MacMullen and E. N. Lane (eds.). *Paganism and Christianity 100–425 c.e.: A Sourcebook.* Minneapolis: Fortress, 1992.

A useful collection of translations of primary sources, arranged by topic, to elucidate the relationship between paganism and Christianity in the early church. Not only are the literary sources included but there are translations of not readily available inscriptions, besides papyri, etc.

453 A. J. Malherbe. *Moral Exhortation, A Greco-Roman Sourcebook.* LEC 4. Philadelphia: Westminster, 1986.

An invaluable anthology of primary sources illustrating Greco-Roman attitudes toward a large variety of moral issues.

454 M. W. Meyer (ed.). *The Ancient Mysteries: A Sourcebook— Sacred Texts of the Mystery Religions of the Ancient Mediterranean World.* San Francisco: Harper & Row, 1987.

A fine collection of primary sources in translation, giving a useful set of texts by which to study mystery religions (although their relevance for the New Testament is probably marginal).

455 B. P. Reardon (ed.). *Collected Ancient Greek Novels.* Berkeley: University of California Press, 1989.

> English translations of all of the major texts and fragments of the Greek novelists, including introductions and bibliographies. One can see for oneself that the New Testament is not a novel.

456 D. G. Rice and J. E. Stambaugh (eds.). *Sources for the Study of Greek Religion.* SBLSBS 14. Missoula: Scholars Press, 1979.

> A very important collection of primary sources from a large range of Greek sources both literary and nonliterary in English translation.

13.1.4 Early Church Fathers, Apocrypha, and Pseudepigrapha

457 *Apostolic Fathers.* 2 vols. LCL. Cambridge: Harvard University Press/London: Heinemann.

> Standard translation including Greek text and critical notes. Old but still useful.

458 J. B. Lightfoot. *The Apostolic Fathers.* Edited by J. R. Harmer. London: Macmillan, 1891. Revised by M. W. Holmes: Peabody: Hendrickson, 1990.

> Standard English translations. Lightfoot edited a much more detailed set of Greek texts of many of these authors (*The Apostolic Fathers: Clement, Ignatius, and Polycarp.* 2 parts, 5 vols. London: Macmillan, 1889–90. Reprinted Peabody: Hendrickson, 1989). The volumes are difficult to use, but potentially useful.

459 J. K. Elliott (ed.). *The Apocryphal New Testament: A Collection of Apocryphal Christian Literature in an English Translation.* Oxford: Clarendon, 1993.

> This is meant to be the completely revised edition of M. R. James's *The Apocryphal New Testament.* Oxford: Oxford University Press, 1924. Revised edition: 1953. It is actually a much more complete and consistent presentation of significant texts for New Testament study (Elliott acknowledges the problem of definition regarding apocrypha).

460 H. M. Gwatkin. *Selections from Early Writers Illustrative of Church History to the Time of Constantine.* London: Macmillan, 1937.

The texts are not complete, but there is a highly useful set of facing page Latin or Greek and English selections.

461 E. Hennecke (ed.). *New Testament Apocrypha.* Edited by W. Schneemelcher. Translated by R. McL. Wilson et al. 2 vols. Philadelphia: Westminster/London: Lutterworth, 1963, 1965. Second edition: Louisville: Westminster/John Knox/ Cambridge: J. Clarke, 1990, 1991. Original title: *Neutestamentliche Apokryphen.* 2 vols. Tübingen: Mohr-Siebeck, 1959, 1964. Fifth edition: 1988.

Standard work, with many helpful introductions. This work cannot be ignored.

13.2 Secondary Sources

13.2.1 General Reference Tools

Most of these sources contain important summary-style essays, with useful bibliography. Although some of the classical sources are dated, many are still valuable for their exposition. A whole range of secondary sources that do not concern themselves with the New Testament in a significant way are not referred to below. They can be accessed through the sources listed. However, the resources below should be more than adequate for an introduction to the subject and its literature.

462 J. Boardman, J. Griffin, and O. Murray (eds.). *The Oxford History of the Classical World.* New York/Oxford: Oxford University Press, 1986.

Included are several chapters on the hellenistic world, including S. Price on hellenistic history (pp. 315–37), R. L. Fox on hellenistic culture and literature (pp. 338–64), and J. Barnes on hellenistic philosophy and science (pp. 365–86). The entire volume is worth reading, however.

463 *Cambridge Ancient History.* 11 vols. Edited by J. B. Bury et al. Cambridge: Cambridge University Press, 1924–36.

Especially relevant are vol. 7 on the hellenistic monarchies and vols. 8–10 on various dimensions of Roman civilization.

464 C. A. Evans. *Noncanonical Writings and New Testament Interpretation.* Peabody: Hendrickson, 1992.

A highly valuable resource, especially for bibliography. There are useful discussions and bibliographies of primary and secondary literature for the Old and New Testament apocrypha and pseudepigrapha, Dead Sea scrolls, Septuagint, Philo and Josephus, rabbinic literature, early church fathers, gnostic writings, and the papyri, plus a few others.

465 E. Ferguson. *Backgrounds of Early Christianity.* Grand Rapids: Eerdmans, 1987. Second edition: 1993.

Probably the best single volume introduction to the background of the New Testament. Various topics have brief exposition and relevant primary and secondary bibliography. His areas of expertise are evident from his discussions, so don't expect the last word on every topic.

466 N. G. L. Hammond and H. H. Scullard (eds.). *The Oxford Classical Dictionary.* Oxford: Clarendon, 1949 (edited by M. O. B. Caspari [Cary], A. D. Nock, et al.). Second edition: 1970.

Standard reference tool. Many obscurities can be clarified with this book.

467 H. Temporini and W. Haase (eds.). *Aufstieg und Niedergang der römischen Welt.* Berlin/New York: de Gruyter, 1972–.

Ongoing series with volumes devoted to the Greco-Roman world and the New Testament, as well as other topics in the ancient world. Quality and length vary significantly. The price makes it almost beyond anyone's reach, so one should not be surprised if the local library does not have it.

13.2.2 Historical Surveys of the Greco-Roman World

These are surveys of the historical periods just before and contemporary with the emergence of Christianity. Serious students will want to supplement these with more detailed treatments of specific topics.

468 W. H. C. Frend. *The Rise of Christianity.* London: Darton, Longman, and Todd/Philadelphia: Fortress, 1984.

Part 1 on Jews and Christians and part 2 on Christianity and the Roman empire are particularly relevant, as Frend traces the development of Christianity out of Judaism and its flourishing in the atmosphere of the Roman world.

469 R. M. Grant. *Augustus to Constantine: The Rise and Triumph of Christianity in the Roman World.* New York/London/San Francisco: Harper & Row, 1970. Revised edition: 1990.

An excellent historical development of early Christianity in the Roman context. The first two parts focus on the emergence of Christianity and its growth and development in the second century.

470 P. Green. *Alexander to Actium: The Historical Evolution of the Hellenistic Age.* Berkeley: University of California Press, 1990.

A massive treatment of the historical background of the hellenistic period, from Alexander to the battle of Actium, which established Octavian's supremacy. Green has several interesting things to say about the spread of Greco-Roman influence in the east. This sets the stage for the New Testament era.

471 F. Millar. *The Roman Near East 31 B.C–A.D. 337.* Cambridge: Harvard University Press, 1993.

A recent treatment of the social and cultural history of the eastern part of the Roman empire, appreciating its diverse complexity. One of the strengths of the book is the perspective it gives to the various religious and ethnic groups within the several subdivisions of the region, all in terms of Greek culture and Roman dominance.

472 E. T. Salmon. *A History of the Roman World 30 B.C. to A.D. 138.* London/New York: Routledge, 1944. Sixth edition: 1968.

An enduring history of the period in which Christianity emerged. It is interesting to note that the author disputes Claudius's edict as caused by dispute over Christ, while accepting Paul's Roman citizenship.

473 C. G. Starr. *A History of the Ancient World*. New York/Oxford: Oxford University Press, 1965. Fourth edition: 1991.

One of the best comprehensive histories of the ancient world, with plenty of detail and not just bland generalizations and sweeping inclusive statements. Particularly useful are sections on the broadening of Greece (VI), the rise of Rome (VII), the consolidation of Roman rule (VIII), and the era of Eurasian stability (IX).

13.2.3 Greco-Roman Society and Institutions Relevant to the New Testament

Greco-Roman society was highly complex, involving a variety of religious, philosophical, racial, cultural, ethnic, and economic factors, among others. Much has come to light in recent years and the student would do well to consult some of the larger and more recent volumes in this area.

13.2.3.1 GENERAL DISCUSSIONS

474 H. Conzelmann. *Gentiles—Jews—Christians: Polemics and Apologetics in the Greco-Roman Era*. Translated by M. E. Boring. Minneapolis: Fortress, 1992. Original title: *Heiden—Juden—Christen: Auseinandersetzungen in der Literatur der hellenistisch-römischen Zeit*. Tübingen: Mohr-Siebeck, 1981.

An interesting and provocative accumulation of primary texts with interpretation regarding the multifaceted relationships among these various groups in the Greco-Roman world. The extent of the author's work in gathering together such sources is astounding. It well illustrates how much the Jewish people were a part of the much larger world of the first century.

475 A. Deissmann. *Light from the Ancient East: The New Testament Illustrated by Recently Discovered Texts of the Graeco-Roman World*. Translated by L. R. M. Strachan. New York: Harper & Row/London: Hodder and Stoughton, 1910. Second edition: New York: Doran/London: Hodder and Stoughton, 1927. Reprinted Grand Rapids: Baker, 1978. Original title: *Licht vom Osten*. Tübingen: Mohr, 1908, second-third edition 1909, fourth edition 1923.

A classic study by one of the first to recognize the importance of the recently discovered papyri and the inscriptions for study of the world of the New Testament in its many dimensions. Many primary texts are included, with translation and annotations. The volume is still very valuable for study and should not be neglected.

476 S. Safrai and M. Stern (eds.). *Compendium Rerum Iudaicarum ad Novum Testamentum*. Assen: Van Gorcum, 1974–.

The first two volumes, entitled *The Jewish People in the First Century* (1974, 1976), are particularly useful for questions of New Testament introduction, containing numerous articles on background issues such as historical geography, political history, and social, cultural, and religious life and institutions.

477 W. W. Tarn. *Hellenistic Civilisation*. London: Edward Arnold, 1927. Third edition with G. T. Griffith: 1952.

A standard work, but one that must be used cautiously, since recent scholarship is calling several of their conclusions into question. There are chapters on Judaism and on hellenistic religion.

478 F. W. Walbank. *The Hellenistic World*. Glasgow: Collins Fontana, 1981. Revised edition: 1992.

The entire book is worth reading for an overview of the subject, but the chapters on religious developments (pp. 209–26) and the arrival of Rome (pp. 227–51) are a must. Included is an excellent short bibliography.

13.2.3.2 GREEK AND HELLENISTIC BACKGROUND TO THE NEW TESTAMENT

This is a huge topic with a large amount of primary and secondary literature available.

479 A. Andrewes. *Greek Society*. Harmondsworth: Penguin, 1967.

Although the period dealt with predates the New Testament, the social-structure analysis is useful for understanding the background to the New Testament.

480 T. Engberg-Pedersen (ed.). *Paul in his Hellenistic Context.* Minneapolis: Fortress/Edinburgh: T. & T. Clark, 1994.

A diverse collection of essays on a number of topics. Some are more detailed and useful than others.

481 M. I. Finley (ed.). *The Legacy of Greece: A New Appraisal.* New York/Oxford: Oxford University Press, 1984.

A completely new version of a book by the same title that appeared in 1921. This is a worthy replacement. Various dimensions of the Greek world are written on by recognized experts, placing them in their proper context. Of importance to New Testament study are chapters on "Education and Rhetoric" by H. I. Marrou (pp. 185–201), "Greek Culture and the Jews" by A. Momigliano (pp. 325–46), and "Greek Philosophy and Christianity" by A. H. Armstrong (pp. 347–75).

482 M. Hengel. *Judaism and Hellenism: Studies in their Encounter during the Early Hellenistic Period.* 2 vols. Translated by J. Bowden. Philadelphia: Fortress/London: SCM, 1974. Original title: *Judentum und Hellenismus: Studien zu ihrer Begegnung unter besonderer Berücksichtigung Palästinas bis zur Mitte des 2 Jh.s v.Chr.* WUNT 10. Tübingen: Mohr-Siebeck, 1969. Second edition: 1973.

A classic study, and one not yet successfully refuted, though many have tried. Hengel proves his case that it is impossible to try to speak of Judaism apart from hellenism. He marshals plenty of evidence to counter presuppositions to the contrary. This is must reading to understand the background of the New Testament.

483 M. Hengel. *Jews, Greeks, and Barbarians: Aspects of the Hellenization of Judaism in the Pre-Christian Period.* Translated by J. Bowden. Philadelphia: Fortress/London: SCM, 1980. Original title: *Juden, Griechen, und Barbaren: Aspekte der Hellenisierung des Judentums in vorchristlicher Zeit.* SB 76. Stuttgart: Katholisches Bibelwerk, 1976.

A continuation of the case made in *Judaism and Hellenism*, including discussion of the Diaspora.

484 M. Hengel. *The 'Hellenization' of Judaea in the First Century after Christ.* Philadelphia: Trinity Press International/

London: SCM, 1989. Original title: "Zum Problem der 'Hellenisierung' Judäas im 1. Jahrhundert nach Christus" (1989). Further support for Hengel's position in *Judaism and Hellenism*, that there can be no rigid lines dividing Judaism from Hellenism. See also *Between Jesus and Paul: Studies in the Earliest History of Christianity*. Translated by J. Bowden. Philadelphia: Fortress/London: SCM, 1983.

485 C. C. Hill. *Hebrews and Hellenists: Reappraising Division within the Earliest Church*. Minneapolis: Fortress, 1992.

Hill explores the implications of the early church being divided along linguistic, cultural, and social lines. Some think that he has overplayed the contrasts.

486 H. Hoehner. *Herod Antipas*. SNTSMS 17. Cambridge: Cambridge University Press, 1972.

Well-documented and researched study of one of the Herods that gives insight into the larger Greco-Roman world. The standard work on the subject.

487 P. W. van der Horst and G. Mussies. *Studies on the Hellenistic Background of the New Testament*. Utrechtse Theologische Reeks 10. Utrecht: Faculteit der Godgeleerdheid, 1990.

A varied collection of essays, many of which are insightful in their dealing with various pagan sources and their possible illustration of aspects of Christianity. Gives an idea of the kind of technical work that can and needs to be done. Van der Horst is expert in this area.

488 W. Jaeger. *Early Christianity and Greek Paideia*. Cambridge/London: Harvard University Press, 1960.

The author of the definitive study of Greek paideia (*Paideia: The Ideals of Greek Culture*. 3 vols. Oxford: Clarendon, 1939–45) applies his results to early Christianity. He argues that there was a mutually fruitful interaction between Christianity and hellenic culture that allowed Christianity to develop, as well as promoting a Christianized hellenic culture.

489 A. H. M. Jones. *The Herods of Judaea*. Oxford: Clarendon, 1938.

A brief but informative study of the Herods, although lacking much reference to primary (or secondary) sources.

490 H. Maccoby. *Paul and Hellenism*. Philadelphia: Trinity Press International/London: SCM, 1991.

Maccoby argues a controversial position that the major influences upon Paul were not the traditional Jewish ones but more Greco-Roman, including the mystery religions and gnosticism. Paul is consequently seen to be quite a creative force in the development of Christian thought. The volume includes interesting discussion of the Greco-Roman world.

491 B. F. Meyer. *The Early Christians: Their World Mission and Self-Discovery*. GNS 16. Wilmington, Del.: Michael Glazier, 1986.

A social study of the context of earliest Christianity and its theological implications. Claims that the launching of the Gentile mission of the early church gave the church its unique identity and initiated the dialectic between its past in Judaism and future as a world-wide mission.

492 J. D. Newsome. *Greeks, Romans, Jews: Currents of Culture and Belief in the New Testament World*. Philadelphia: Trinity Press International, 1992.

A reasonably thorough discussion of hellenistic influence on the Jews. Not as optimistic as Hengel (see nos. 348/482, 484) regarding how hellenistic Judaism was in the first century, the study is not as thorough as Hengel's and fails to make some important distinctions.

493 C. J. Roetzel. *The World That Shaped the New Testament*. Atlanta: John Knox, 1985.

A small but useful volume that focuses on the political and social structures of the Roman empire and their impact on early Christianity. Offers also a helpful discussion of the kinds of interpretation of religious texts in Judaism as a background for understanding how the early Christians interpreted Scripture.

494 E. P. Sanders (ed.). *Jewish and Christian Self-Definition*. I. *The Shaping of Christianity in the Second and Third Centuries*. III. Edited with B. F. Meyer. *Self-Definition in the*

Greco-Roman World. Philadelphia: Fortress/London: SCM, 1980, 1982.

Classic collections of essays. There are insightful and compact essays on a number of the key issues facing interpretation of the New Testament in the context of the world of its time. Vol. 3 is especially important for establishing the religious and philosophical background to the New Testament.

495 V. A. Tcherikover. *Hellenistic Civilization and the Jews.* Philadelphia: Jewish Publication Society of America, 1959.

In many ways superseded by Hengel's work (nos. 348/ 482), although still a useful compendium of information.

13.2.3.3 ROMAN BACKGROUND TO THE NEW TESTAMENT

496 L. Alexander (ed.). *Images of Empire.* JSOT Supplement Series 122. Sheffield: JSOT Press, 1991.

Essays exploring how the Roman empire was perceived by various groups within it.

497 S. S. Bartchy. *First-Century Slavery and 1 Corinthians 7:21.* SBLDS 11. Atlanta: Scholars Press, 1973.

Pp. 37–125 deal with the conventions of first-century slavery in the Greco-Roman world. Careful, worthwhile assessment.

498 K. Christ. *The Romans: An Introduction to their History and Civilization.* Translated by C. Holme. Berkeley: University of California Press, 1984.

Especially helpful in describing the classes in Roman society, Roman law, and the competing religions of the empire in the beginning centuries of the Christian era.

499 F. C. Grant. *Roman Hellenism and the New Testament.* New York: Scribners, 1962.

The New Testament is placed within its Roman hellenistic environment. See pp. 1–80 on Roman religion. Older work, but well researched and useful.

500 E. L. Luttwak. *The Grand Strategy of the Roman Empire: From the First Century A.D. to the Third.* Baltimore/London: Johns Hopkins University Press, 1976.

Describes the social and political concerns of the empire as Christianity was emerging from Palestine and becoming an empire-wide religion.

501 D. B. Martin. *Slavery as Salvation: The Metaphor of Slavery in Pauline Christianity.* New Haven/London: Yale University Press, 1990.

An excellent survey of the many complexities regarding slavery in the Greco-Roman world, with exploration of how slavery language was taken up especially in Pauline Christianity. The author widely refers to epigraphic sources to establish his position that the imagery has traditionally not been understood in its rightful social context. See also K. R. Bradley. *Slaves and Masters in the Roman Empire: A Study in Social Control.* Belgium: Editions Latomus, 1982. Reprinted New York/Oxford: Oxford University Press, 1987, a very revealing study about the abject conditions of slavery in the ancient world, in which the lives of the slaves were dominated by their masters in almost every way.

502 A. N. Sherwin-White. *Roman Society and Roman Law in the New Testament.* Oxford: Clarendon, 1963.

Still a very important study of the relationship between Roman law and society and the New Testament as written by a classical historian. He seems more willing to give the New Testament documents the benefit of the historical doubt than many New Testament scholars.

503 E. M. Smallwood. *The Jews under Roman Rule: From Pompey to Diocletian.* SJLA 20. Leiden: Brill, 1976.

Standard treatment of the subject, complete with references to primary literature. Helpful for understanding the world from which Christianity emerged.

504 C. G. Starr. *The Ancient Romans.* New York: Oxford University Press, 1971.

Useful, brief chapter on the rise and spread of Christianity as part of the Roman world, written by an acknowledged master of telling the story of the ancient world. See also A. Watson. *The Law of the Ancient Romans.* Dallas: Southern Methodist University Press, 1970, for an informed discussion of Roman law by a law professor. Although the New Testament is not specifically treated, there are manifest implications suggested by the text.

505 C. Wells. *The Roman Empire.* Stanford, Calif.: Stanford University Press, 1984.

Describes the Roman empire from the days just prior to Augustus (44 B.C.) until ca. A.D. 235. Describes life in the city, countryside, and army camps of the Romans.

13.2.4 Greco-Roman Religion and the New Testament

506 D. E. Aune. *Prophecy in Early Christianity and the Ancient Mediterranean World.* Grand Rapids: Eerdmans, 1983.

The standard treatment of the subject, which resorts not to simple assertion but to thorough analysis of the ancient literature. The survey of ancient literature is worth looking at alone.

507 W. Burkert. *Greek Religion.* Translated by J. Raffan. Cambridge: Harvard University Press, 1985. Original title: *Griechische Religion der archaischen und klassischen Epoche.* Stuttgart: Kohlhammer, 1977.

Of direct relevance to the study of the New Testament are chapters on rituals such as sacrifice (part II), the various gods (part III), and mysteries including Bacchic ones (part VI). There are numerous suggestive sections interspersed (e.g., on oaths, pp. 250–54).

508 R. L. Fox. *Pagans and Christians.* Perennial Library. New York/London/San Francisco: Harper & Row, 1987.

A most useful and celebrated resource on the pagan religion and how early Christians interfaced with and competed against often strange religious expressions.

509 J. Finegan. *Myth and Mystery: An Introduction to the Pagan Religions of the Biblical World.* Grand Rapids: Baker, 1989.

An excellent work that focuses on Mesopotamian religions, Gnosticism, the Egyptian religions, Greek and Roman deities, and also the later Mandaean and Manichaean religions.

510 T. R. Glover. *The Conflict of Religions in the Early Roman Empire.* London: Methuen, 1909.

A classic study by an influential thinker on the subject of the relationship of Christianity to its religious environment.

511 R. M. Grant. *Gods and the One God*. LEC 1. Philadelphia: Westminster, 1986. British edition: *Gods and the One God: Christian Theology in the Graeco-Roman World*. London: SPCK, 1986.

A useful introduction to the religious environment of the hellenistic world and how early Christianity responded to the challenges that this presented in terms of such things as monotheism and Christology.

512 W. K. C. Guthrie. *The Greeks and their Gods*. Boston: Beacon/London: Methuen, 1950.

The classic study by the well-known classicist, who explores the relationship between the Greeks and their gods, arguing for the distinctiveness of the Greek pantheon. Individual gods and goddesses are discussed, including many of the lesser known ones, from the classical period.

513 P. W. van der Horst. *Hellenism—Judaism—Christianity: Essays on their Interaction*. CBET 8. Kampen: Kok Pharos, 1994.

A number of recent essays that illustrate the relationship between hellenism, Judaism, and Christianity, including discussion of Jewish epitaphs in Greek, the godfearers, and the altar to the unknown God, among many others. Van der Horst does an excellent job of illustrating the complex religious environment of the Greco-Roman world.

514 G. S. Kirk. *The Nature of Greek Myths*. Harmondsworth: Penguin, 1974.

A hard-headed approach to myth that attempts to clarify many of the loose definitions and theories of origins. Important reading for students of the New Testament.

515 R. MacMullen. *Paganism in the Roman Empire*. New Haven/London: Yale University Press, 1981.

An important volume for elucidating the religious milieu of early Christianity by a significant scholar of the Greco-Roman world.

516 L. H. Martin. *Hellenistic Religions: An Introduction.* New York/Oxford: Oxford University Press, 1987.

Basic introductions and summaries, with selective bibliographies after each section.

517 G. Murray. *Five Stages of Greek Religion.* London: Watts, 1935.

See especially chapter 4 on "The Failure of Nerve," the way in which Murray characterizes what led to the eventual decline of Greek religious thought.

518 A. D. Nock. *Conversion.* Oxford: Oxford University Press, 1933.

This classic study on the psychology of religious conversion from the third century B.C. to the fourth century A.D. traces the conflict between philosophy and religion, illustrating the increasing intolerance of religion. Many of the author's papers were gathered together in *Essays on Religion and the Ancient World.* Edited by Z. Stewart. 2 vols. Cambridge: Harvard University Press, 1972.

519 R. M. Ogilvie. *The Romans and their Gods in the Age of Augustus.* London: Chatto and Windus, 1969.

A brief but up-to-date conspectus on Roman religion at the time of the New Testament, discussing such issues as prayer, sacrifice, divination, and private religion.

520 H. J. Rose. *Religion in Greece and Rome.* New York: Harper and Brothers, 1959.

Originally published as two separate volumes on Greek religion (1946) and Roman religion (1948), this is arguably still the best summary of religion in Greece and Rome available in English.

13.2.5 Greco-Roman Philosophy and the New Testament

In the New Testament, although explicit references to Greco-Roman philosophy are few, apparent parallels with Greco-Roman philosophy appear in some key context, and problems in the early church may well have had philosophical underpinnings. Nevertheless, it is difficult to determine the exact relationship between philosophy and the New Testament.

521 D. L. Balch, E. Ferguson, and W. A. Meeks (eds.). *Greeks, Romans, and Christians: Essays in Honor of A. J. Malherbe.* Minneapolis: Fortress, 1990.

A worthy collection of essays, all focused upon the relation between the New Testament and its hellenistic literary and rhetorical, religious, and philosophical milieu. Most of the authors make an attempt to relate the two. The excellent contributions are too many to list. The section on philosophy is particularly insightful.

522 G. Bowersock. *Approaches to the Second Sophistic.* University Park, Penn.: American Philological Association, 1974.

Essays on the sophists by scholars writing in their areas of expertise. Excellent selective bibliography in Appendix I.

523 J. L. Kinneavy. *Greek Rhetorical Origins of Christian Faith: An Inquiry.* New York: Oxford University Press, 1987.

An interesting and provocative (if unconvincing) analysis of the concept of faith as originating in Greek rhetoric and philosophy. The major flaws of the study are its reliance upon the etymological argument and the confusion of word and concept.

524 A. J. Malherbe. *Paul and the Popular Philosophers.* Minneapolis: Fortress, 1989.

Malherbe collects a number of previously published significant essays that illustrate the background of the New Testament against popular thought of the time, including especially Cynic philosophy and the use of diatribe.

525 J. M. Rist. *Stoic Philosophy.* Cambridge: Cambridge University Press, 1977.

Standard exposition of Stoic philosophy.

13.2.6 Greco-Roman Literature Relevant to the New Testament

See the discussion of epistolary form as well (Part 1, chapter 3.3.7).

13.2.6.1 SUMMARIES AND DESCRIPTIONS

526 D. E. Aune (ed.). *Greco-Roman Literature and the New Testament.* SBLSBS 21. Atlanta: Scholars Press, 1988.

Included are important articles on the diatribe by S. K. Stowers (pp. 71–84), the ancient Greek letter by J. L.

White (pp. 85–106), Greco-Roman biography by Aune (pp. 107–26), and the Greek novel by R. F. Hock (pp. 127–46).

527 R. A. Burridge. *What are the Gospels? A Comparison with Graeco-Roman Biography.* SNTSMS 70. Cambridge: Cambridge University Press, 1992.

A capable defense of the hypothesis that the Gospels are Graeco-Roman "lives." The bibliography refers to the important earlier sources.

528 A. Dihle. *Greek and Latin Literature of the Roman Empire: From Augustus to Justinian.* London/New York: Routledge, 1994. Original: Munich: Beck, 1989.

See pp. 203–12 for Christian literature, although finding out about other literature of the time is very worthwhile.

529 D. L. Dungan and D. R. Cartlidge. *Sourcebook of Texts for the Comparative Study of the Gospels.* Missoula: Scholars Press, 1973. Revised edition: *Documents for the Study of the Gospels.* Philadelphia: Fortress/London: Collins, 1980.

An excellent collection of ancient noncanonical sources that have parallels with the canonical literature or help explain parts of that literature or events of the New Testament. Parallels in gospel genre, miracle stories, teachings, sacraments, apocalyptic, and ascension stories are included.

530 K. J. Dover et al. *Ancient Greek Literature.* Oxford: Oxford University Press, 1980.

Reference should be made to Dover's chapter on classical oratory (pp. 122–33), J. Griffin's on Greek literature from 300–50 B.C. (pp. 134–54), and E. L. Bowie's on Greek literature after 50 B.C. (pp. 155–76).

531 S. E. Porter. "The 'We' Passages." Pp. 545–74 in D. W. J. Gill and C. Gempf (eds.). *The Book of Acts in its First Century Setting.* II. *The Book of Acts in its Graeco-Roman Setting.* Grand Rapids: Eerdmans/Carlisle: Paternoster, 1994.

Summary and analysis of opinions on the genre of Acts. New perspective on the "we" passages as an independent source.

532 S. K. Stowers. *The Diatribe and Paul's Letter to the Romans.* SBLDS 57. Chico: Scholars Press, 1981.

The most comprehensive treatment of diatribe to date, and a necessary revival of the subject since Bultmann's classic (though often unread) work, *Der Stil der paulinischen Predigt und die kynisch-stoische Diatribe.* Göttingen: Vandenhoeck & Ruprecht, 1910. Reprint in FRLANT: 1984.

533 B. W. Winter and A. D. Clarke (eds.). *The Book of Acts in its First Century Setting.* I. *The Book of Acts in its Ancient Literary Setting.* Grand Rapids: Eerdmans/Carlisle: Paternoster, 1993.

A compendium of essays on various topics related to Acts, including R. Bauckham on the Acts of Paul (pp. 105–52), D. W. Palmer on the ancient historical monograph (pp. 1–29), and L. C. A. Alexander on intellectual biography (pp. 31–63).

13.2.6.2 JOSEPHUS AND THE NEW TESTAMENT

534 P. Bilde. *Flavius Josephus between Jerusalem and Rome: His Life, his Works, and their Importance.* JSPSup 2. Sheffield: JSOT Press, 1988.

An overview of Josephus and his writings.

535 L. H. Feldman and G. Hata (eds.). *Josephus, the Bible, and History.* Detroit: Wayne State University Press, 1989.

Important collection of essays by prominent Jewish scholars over the contributions and reliability of Josephus when he describes matters related to the canon, various sects of Judaism, revolutionary parties in the first century, and the land of Israel. Insists on caution when reading Josephus as a historical resource.

536 P. L. Maier (trans. and ed.). *Josephus: The Essential Writings.* Grand Rapids: Kregel, 1988.

A welcome newer translation of Jewish Antiquities and the Jewish War. Contains some helpful diagrams and illustrations.

537 S. Mason. *Josephus and the New Testament.* Peabody: Hendrickson, 1992.

A very useful discussion of the relationship between Josephus and the New Testament. Mason has salutary words about how much and in what way Josephus may legitimately be used in New Testament research, followed by discussion of his career and writings. He concludes with a chapter on Josephus and Luke–Acts, especially comparing the two as historians.

538 T. Rajak. *Josephus: The Historian and his Society*. London: Duckworth/Philadelphia: Fortress, 1983.

A thorough study of Josephus, which attempts to place him within his larger historical and linguistic context.

539 G. E. Sterling. *Historiography and Self-Definition: Josephus, Luke–Acts and Apologetic Historiography*. NovTSup 64. Leiden: Brill, 1992.

An attempt to establish apologetic historiography as a genre. Doubtful whether the attempt is entirely successful, but a lot of literature is surveyed.

540 H. St. J. Thackeray et al. (trans. and ed.). *Josephus.* 10 vols. LCL. Cambridge: Harvard University Press/London: Heinemann.

Still the standard translation and the basic resource on Josephus for research students.

541 W. Whiston (trans.). *The Works of Josephus: Complete and Unabridged.* 1736. Revised edition: Peabody: Hendrickson, 1987.

A helpful edition that incorporates the Loeb Classical Library numbering system with that of the original text. Additional notes clarify the text and very useful indexes are added.

542 G. A. Williamson (trans. and ed.). *Josephus: The Jewish War.* Penguin Classics. London: Penguin, 1959. Revised edition: 1970. Introductory and editorial comments by E. M. Smallwood: 1981.

A readable translation with helpful introduction and additional sections and charts at the end of the book that focus on the Greco-Roman context of first-century Judaism.

13.2.6.3 OTHER INDIVIDUAL AUTHORS
RELEVANT TO THE NEW TESTAMENT

543 H. D. Betz (ed.). *Plutarch's Theological Writings and Early Christian Literature.* SCHNT 3. Leiden: Brill, 1975.
Excellent resource.

544 H. D. Betz (ed.). *Plutarch's Ethical Writings and Early Christian Literature.* SCHNT 4. Leiden: Brill, 1978.
Excellent resource.

545 G. Mussies. *Dio Chrysostom and the New Testament: Parallels Collected.* Leiden: Brill, 1971.

546 R. Williamson. *Philo and the Epistle to the Hebrews.* ALGHJ 4. Leiden: Brill, 1970.

547 C. D. Yonge (trans.). *The Works of Philo: Complete and Unabridged.* 1854–55. Revised edition: Peabody: Hendrickson, 1993.
Useful and readable. Helpful indexes. Does not take the place of the Loeb Classical Library edition, but a welcome translation nevertheless.

14

Gnosticism

The major critical question regarding gnosticism is the extent of its relationship with Christianity. In other words, was gnosticism a religious-philosophical phenomenon that emerged later than Christianity, quite possibly influenced by it, did it emerge independently at the same time as Christianity, or did it emerge at the same time or even before Christianity, with some sort of mutual influence? Whereas earlier in this century there was much optimism for Christianity having been influenced by gnosticism (late sources were often invoked to make this case), recent discussion tends more toward the view that there was at best mutual influence. Many still maintain only that gnosticism was influenced by Christianity. The Nag Hammadi documents are the single largest collection of gnostic documents, written in Coptic. The documents themselves date to the third century, but debate revolves around whether they reflect earlier traditions that may have influenced the New Testament. There are several Greek fragments that apparently come from the Gospel of Thomas (P. Oxyrhynchus 1, 654, 655). Some of the New Testament letters may reflect opponents with gnostic tendencies.

14.1 Primary Sources

548 W. Barnstone (ed.). *The Other Bible*. New York: Harper & Row, 1984.

Collection of ancient esoteric texts from the Judeo-Christian community that are not found in the Christian biblical canon. Helpful introductions to a wide range of writings including a number of gnostic texts.

549 A. Guillaumont et al. (trans.). *The Gospel according to Thomas*. New York/Evanston: Harper & Row/Leiden: Brill, 1959.

Standard facing page translation of the most important of the finds from Nag Hammadi. The complete library is available from Brill.

550 B. Layton. *The Gnostic Scriptures: A New Translation, with Annotations and Introductions.* Garden City: Doubleday/London: SCM, 1987.

Careful introductory chapter (pp. 5–21), recent translation, and helpful notes for clarifying the meaning of the text. Almost a standard reference from the time of its publication.

551 J. M. Robinson (ed.). *The Nag Hammadi Library in English.* New York: Harper & Row/Leiden: Brill, 1977. Third revised edition: 1988.

Standard translation of the Nag Hammadi documents and helpful notes about each document by competent scholars. Despite some vociferous claims otherwise, there is debate over the value of these documents for understanding the New Testament. Those who argue that gnosticism was present in the first century find greater value in this collection than those who view it as a second-century development. Many scholars argue for an "incipient gnosticism" in the first century.

14.2 Secondary Analyses

552 C. A. Evans, R. L. Webb, and R. A. Wiebe. *Nag Hammadi Texts and the Bible: A Synopsis and Index*. NTTS 18. Leiden: Brill, 1993.

Excellent reference tool.

553 G. Filoramo. *A History of Gnosticism*. Translated by A. Alcock. Cambridge, Mass./Oxford: Blackwell, 1990. Original title: *L'attesa della fine: Soria della gnosi.* Gius, Laterza, and Figli.

Careful analysis of the emergence of gnosticism and its relations to early Christianity.

554 J. Goehring, C. Hedrick, J. Sanders, and H. D. Betz (eds.). *Gnosticism and the Early Christian World.* Sonoma, Calif.: Polebridge, 1990.

One of two volumes honoring J. M. Robinson. The essays in both volumes probe into primary gnostic texts and answer the questions of what gave rise to them and how do they relate to New Testament texts.

555 C. W. Hedrick and R. Hodgson, Jr. (eds.). *Nag Hammadi, Gnosticism, and Early Christianity.* Peabody: Hendrickson, 1986.

A useful collection of essays that discuss the origins and relations of gnosticism as found in the Nag Hammadi texts to Christianity. Useful for the nonspecialist and for the advanced student. Primary contributors include G. MacRae, H. Koester, B. Layton, E. Pagels, P. Perkins, B. Pearson, J. M. Robinson, J. D. Turner, F. Wisse, and others.

556 H. Jonas. *The Gnostic Religion: The Message of the Alien God and the Beginnings of Christianity.* Boston: Beacon, 1958. Reprinted London/New York: Routledge, 1992.

For years the standard text on the origin and beliefs of gnosticism. Still valuable resource even though much of the material is dated.

557 G. W. MacRae. *Studies in the New Testament and Gnosticism.* Edited by D. J. Harrington and S. B. Marrow. GNS 26. Wilmington, Del.: Michael Glazier, 1987.

Several of the late MacRae's most important essays on gnosticism are reprinted here, illustrating his moderate view that Christianity was from the start responding to an incipient form of gnosticism.

558 P. Perkins. *Gnosticism and the New Testament.* Minneapolis: Fortress, 1993.

In the first systematic treatment of the relationship between the gnostic sources and the New Testament in twenty-five years (since Jonas; see no. 560), the author essentially argues for simultaneous development, depicting the early church as an environment full of competing theological interests.

559 B. A. Pearson. *Gnosticism, Judaism, and Egyptian Christianity*. Studies in Antiquity & Christianity. Minneapolis: Fortress, 1990.

560 K. Rudolph. *Gnosis: The Nature and History of an Ancient Religion*. Translated by R. McL. Wilson. Edinburgh: T. & T. Clark, 1983. Original title: *Die Gnosis: Wesen und Geschichte einer spätantiken Religion*. 2 vols. Leipzig: Koehler & Amelang, 1977/Göttingen: Vandenhoeck & Ruprecht, 1978.

A standard exposition of gnosticism, but one that sees it developing quite early.

561 B. Walker. *Gnosticism: Its History and Influence*. Wellingborough, England: Aquarian Press, 1989.

Useful, well written, but not exhaustive.

562 E. M. Yamauchi. *Pre-Christian Gnosticism: A Survey of the Proposed Evidences*. Grand Rapids: Eerdmans/London: Tyndale, 1973.

Yamauchi here argues that gnosticism was at best only incipient and probably later than Christianity. In no case were the two equals struggling with mutual definition. Thus Bultmann's hypothesis is questioned. Well researched and an alternative to several popular but not necessarily correct views.

15

The New Testament and Archaeology

The relationship between the New Testament and archaeology is different from that of the Old Testament and archaeology in several respects, not least because it moves westward rather than eastward. Nevertheless, difficulties abound, since little accessible information for Asia Minor or Greece is relevant for New Testament study. For those areas where there is evidence—such as Galilee—the problems of archaeology still abound. We are past the optimism of a previous generation when archaeology was used apologetically and seen to confirm all of the biblical data. We realize now that archaeological data—like all data—require interpretation. Presuppositions are brought to the task, interpretative models must be utilized, evidence must be carefully weighed, and competing theories must be recognized. The following is a list of some of the more helpful sources in this area.

563 M. Avi-Yonah and E. Stern (eds.). *Encyclopedia of Archaeological Expeditions in the Holy Land.* 4 vols. Englewood Cliffs, N.J.: Prentice-Hall/London: Oxford University Press, 1975–78.

> Standard resource with useful discussions of a vast number of the major expeditions and finds, complete with many pictures and some texts.

564 E. M. Blaiklock and R. K. Harrison (eds.). *The New International Dictionary of Biblical Archaeology.* Grand Rapids: Zondervan, 1983.

A useful tool that is more exhaustive than most in its breadth, but consequently quite limited. Several articles are outdated (the work on Psidian Antioch is based mostly on the earlier work of W. Ramsay, which has been replaced by remarkable finds in recent years), but still a useful tool for basic information.

565 J. H. Charlesworth and W. P. Weaver (eds.). *What Has Archaeology to do with Faith?* Faith and Scholarship Colloquies. Philadelphia: Trinity Press International, 1992.

Four important essays, the first two of which (Charlesworth and J. F. Strange) the beginning student will find helpful for New Testament studies.

566 G. G. Cornfeld. *Archaeology and the Bible: Book by Book.* New York: Harper & Row, 1976.

Most attention is given to the Old Testament and Intertestamental period, but Cornfeld summarizes in a book by book fashion what is known. Several excellent diagrams, pictures, and illustrations.

567 J. Finegan. *The Archaeology of the New Testament: The Life of Jesus and the Beginning of the Early Church.* Princeton: Princeton University Press, 1969. Revised edition: 1992.

Texts and findings with particular application to the New Testament. First edition a bit dated in approach, but the significant revision makes this an excellent resource. Although he does have a brief section on the catacombs of Rome, there is little awareness of what was going on in the rest of the Greco-Roman world as the early Christians extended their ministry beyond Palestine.

568 J. Finegan. *Light from the Ancient Past.* Princeton: Princeton University Press, 1959.

A still useful collection of texts and discussion, but getting older.

569 S. Freyne. *Galilee from Alexander the Great to Hadrian, 323 B.C.E. to 135 C.E.: A Study of Second Temple Judaism.*

Wilmington, Del.: Michael Glazier/Notre Dame: Notre Dame University Press, 1980.

A detailed look at the economic and cultural life of Galilee in the time surrounding the New Testament, concluding that it was more isolated than many have argued. Not all are convinced, especially since he does not consider linguistic factors enough.

570 S. Freyne. *Galilee, Jesus, and the Gospels: Literary Approaches and Historical Investigations.* Philadelphia: Fortress/Dublin: Gill and Macmillan, 1988.

A literary treatment of Galilee, placing more emphasis on the Gospel texts rather than the extrabiblical evidence considered in Freyne's more extensive study.

571 D. W. J. Gill and C. Gempf (eds.). *The Book of Acts in its First Century Setting.* II. *The Book of Acts in its Greco-Roman Setting.* Grand Rapids: Eerdmans/Carlisle: Paternoster, 1994.

A compendium of essays on various topics related to Acts and its Greco-Roman archaeological and cultural setting. Many of the essays are well documented regarding the latest evidence, although several are apologetic.

572 R. K. Harrison (ed.). *Major Cities of the Biblical World.* Nashville: Nelson, 1985.

Brief descriptions of biblical cities, some of them by archaeologists. In any event useful bibliography is provided for further reference.

573 L. I. Levine (ed.). *The Galilee in Late Antiquity.* New York/ Jerusalem: Jewish Theological Seminary of America, 1992.

A useful collection that helps to illuminate the significance and place of Galilee with regard to Christianity, Roman rule, Judaism, language (Greek is strangely neglected), and archaeology. Contributors include D. Edwards, H. C. Kee, A. J. Saldarini, S. Freyne, M. Goodman, L. H. Schiffman, S. J. D. Cohen, E. M. Meyers, and J. F. Strange, among others.

574 W. H. Mare. *The Archaeology of the Jerusalem Area.* Grand Rapids: Baker, 1987.

An excellent resource on the history and archaeological finds in and around Jerusalem. Contains a number of sketches, pictures, archaeologists' reconstructions, and diagrams that are helpful in understanding the events that took place in this ancient city.

575 J. McRay. *Archaeology and the New Testament.* Grand Rapids: Baker, 1991.

This is one of the most useful and well illustrated works of its kind. Produced by a careful scholar, it is readable and its organization (Palestine, Asia Minor, Greece, and Rome) allows it to be used as a textbook on the journeys of Paul. Numerous diagrams and charts.

576 E. M. Meyers and J. F. Strange. *Archaeology, the Rabbis and Early Christianity.* Nashville: Abingdon/London: SCM, 1981.

An exceptionally useful book, since it treats the nonliterary evidence regarding the world of early Christianity. Surveys are included regarding the state of knowledge of various cities in Palestine, the languages in use, and various social institutions such as the synagogue.

577 P. R. S. Mooney. *A Century of Biblical Archaeology.* Louisville: Westminster/John Knox, 1991.

Discussion of the developments in archaeology and its method in this century. He is fairly negative toward the apologetic approach.

578 J. Murphy-O'Connor. *The Holy Land: An Archaeological Guide from Earliest Times to 1700.* New York/Oxford: Oxford University Press, 1980. Third edition: 1992.

A useful tool for exploring Israel in antiquity and even more recently. Useful diagrams and descriptions of biblical sites including a generous collection of New Testament sites. Scholarly but without the heavy jargon and designed to be read by a wide audience. Those visiting Israel today should read it.

579 J. Murphy-O'Connor. *St. Paul's Corinth: Texts and Archaeology.* GNS 6. Michael Glazier Book. Collegeville, Minn.: Liturgical Press, 1983.

Without question the best treatment on ancient Corinth
in print. Excellent treatment of ancient primary texts
that mention Corinth and clarifies a number of passages
that seem strange in the New Testament, namely, the
Corinthians eating before others arrived to celebrate the
Eucharist (1 Corinthians 11). Includes the Gallio text
found at Delphi that dates the time of Paul's ministry in
Corinth.

580 K. N. Schoville. *Biblical Archaeology in Focus.* Grand Rapids: Baker, 1978.

Excellent treatment of Palestine in both the Old Testament and New Testament periods, but decidedly weak on
New Testament sites for Paul's ministry in Greece, Asia
Minor, and Italy as well as the Seven Churches of Asia
Minor. Greco-Roman world receives scant attention. Pictures are generally well done, but again too few and not as
focused as students of New Testament studies would
like.

581 W. H. Stephens. *The New Testament World in Pictures.*
Nashville: Broadman, 1987.

Illustrates with numerous pictures the ancient world of
the New Testament. Descriptions are brief and generally
reliable.

582 M. Taslialan. *Psidian Antioch: The Journeys of St. Paul to
Antioch.* Istanbul: Besyol, 1991.

The most recent description of the excavations going on
at Psidian Antioch by its leading archaeologist and director of the Museum at Yalvac (ancient Antioch). A small
but important investigation of one of the largest and most
significant cities in the Asia Minor interior in the first
century when Paul ministered there. He observes that the
city was as large as or larger than Ephesus.

583 J. A. Thompson. *The Bible and Archaeology.* Grand Rapids:
Eerdmans, 1962. Third edition: 1982.

The volume for years was the standard text in many conservative schools on archaeology and the Bible. Its revision, though heavily favoring the Old Testament, offers a
careful assessment of New Testament sites and historical

information. Well illustrated and valuable for both the Jewish and Greco-Roman context of early Christianity.

584 P. Trebilco. *Jewish Communities in Asia Minor.* SNTSMS 69. Cambridge: Cambridge University Press, 1991.

Documentation through a survey of primary sources.

585 H. T. Vos. *Archaeology of Bible Lands.* Chicago: Moody, 1977.

Not as useful on the New Testament, but has some sections that warrant attention.

586 E. M. Yamauchi. *New Testament Cities in Western Asia Minor: Light from Archaeology on Cities of Paul and the Seven Churches of Revelation.* Grand Rapids: Baker, 1980. British edition: *The Archaeology of New Testament Cities in Western Asia Minor.* London/Glasgow: Pickering & Inglis, 1980.

A small but excellent resource by a competent scholar in the field. Several helpful site diagrams, maps, and pictures are included that make the book even more useful. A good guide for those visiting the ancient sites.

16

General Resources

16.1 Bible Dictionaries and Encyclopedias

Interest in producing Bible dictionaries and encyclopedias has recently increased. Thus most if not all of the established resources of the turn of the century or before are being replaced.

587 G. W. Bromiley (ed.). *The International Standard Bible Encyclopedia*. 4 vols. Grand Rapids: Eerdmans/Exeter: Paternoster, 1979–88.

Revision of the original, J. Orr (ed.). *The International Standard Bible Encyclopaedia*. 5 vols. Chicago/London: Camp, 1915. Revised edition: Chicago: Howard-Severance, 1930.

Among the best of Bible encyclopedias from a conservative standpoint.

588 G. A. Buttrick (ed.). *The Interpreter's Bible Dictionary*. 4 vols. New York/Nashville: Abingdon, 1962. Supplementary Volume edited by K. Crim: 1976.

Older dictionary still of value even though several articles are out of date. The supplement has many useful essays.

589 F. L. Cross (ed.). *The Oxford Dictionary of the Christian Church*. Oxford: Oxford University Press, 1957. Second edition with E. A. Livingstone: 1974.

Standard reference tool.

590 J. D. Douglas et al. (eds.). *The New Bible Dictionary*. Wheaton, Ill.: Tyndale/London: InterVarsity, 1962. Second edition: 1982.

Acceptable one-volume dictionary from conservative perspective.

591 D. N. Freedman (ed.). *The Anchor Bible Dictionary*. 6 vols. New York/London: Doubleday, 1992.

This has become the standard, authoritative Bible dictionary replacing the *Interpreter's Bible Dictionary* (no. 588). Contains many excellent essays that are often foundational for research but also with a few shortcomings. If there is only time to consult one dictionary, this is it.

592 L. Pirot, A. Robert, J. Briend, and E. Cothenet (eds.). *Dictionnaire de la Bible Supplement*. Paris: Letouzey, 1928–.

11 vols. completed by 1991.

593 C. Roth (ed.). *Encyclopedia Judaica*. 16 vols. Jerusalem: Macmillan, 1971–72.

Standard resource.

594 I. Singer (ed.). *The Jewish Encyclopedia*. 12 vols. New York: Funk and Wagnalls, 1901–06.

Now dated since appearance of *Encyclopedia Judaica* (no. 593), although many articles are still of value. Views of early Christianity are less balanced than more recent Jewish scholarship provides.

595 H. S. Gehman (ed.). *The New Westminster Dictionary of the Bible*. Philadelphia: Westminster, 1970.

Brief but informative articles.

596 P. Achtemeier (ed.). *Harper's Bible Dictionary*. San Francisco: Harper & Row, 1985.

This new dictionary replaces M. S. Miller and J. L. Miller (eds.). *Harper's Bible Dictionary*. New York: Harper and Brothers, 1952/London: A. & C. Black, 1954. Eighth edition: New York: Harper & Row, 1973. Highly useful, authoritative, and not unduly compact.

597 J. B. Green and S. McKnight (eds.). *Dictionary of Jesus and the Gospels*. Downers Grove/Leicester: InterVarsity, 1992.

Now a standard specialist dictionary on the topic.

598 J. Hastings (ed.). *A Dictionary of the Bible*. 4 vols. with extra volume. New York: Scribners/Edinburgh: T. & T. Clark, 1898–1902, 1904. Second edition in 2 vols. revised by F. C. Grant and H. H. Rowley: 1963.

An enduring multivolume dictionary that is seriously dated but still worth consulting for its wealth of historical information.

599 J. Hastings (ed.). *A Dictionary of Christ and the Gospels*. 2 vols. New York: Scribners/Edinburgh: T. & T. Clark, 1906, 1908.

600 J. Hastings (ed.). *Dictionary of the Apostolic Church*. 2 vols. New York: Scribners/Edinburgh: T. & T. Clark, 1915, 1918.

Seriously dated, but still worthwhile reading for supplementary information. Many of the conclusions have been replaced, but for its time, a remarkable achievement.

601 G. F. Hawthorne and R. P. Martin (eds.). *Dictionary of Paul and his Letters*. Downers Grove/Leicester: InterVarsity, 1993.

Now a standard specialist dictionary on the topic. Traditional but well argued conclusions.

16.2 Bible Atlases

602 Y. Aharoni and M. Avi-Yonah. *The Macmillan Bible Atlas*. New York: Macmillan/London: Collier-Macmillan, 1968. Third revised edition also with A. F. Rainey and Z. Safrai: 1993.

Arguably the best historical atlas with excellent background information on both the Old and New Testaments. Maps are clear and accurate. Third edition has been completely revised. New Testament portion is limited, but information and the depictions are generally quite accurate.

603 *Atlas of Bible History*. Oxford/Batavia/Sydney: Lion, 1978. Also published as *Eerdmans Atlas of the Bible*. Grand Rapids: Eerdmans, 1978.

Concise and useful for beginning student, but the advanced student will want more.

604 D. Baly. *The Geography of the Bible: A Study in Historical Geography.* New York: Harper and Brothers, 1957. Revised edition: London: Lutterworth, 1974.

Useful maps but information dated.

605 B. J. Beitzel. *The Moody Atlas of Bible Lands.* Chicago: Moody, 1985.

Mostly focuses on Old Testament, but generally careful on the New Testament.

606 J. J. Bimson, J. P. Kane, J. H. Paterson, D. J. Wiseman, and D. R. W. Wood. *New Bible Atlas.* Leicester/Downers Grove: InterVarsity, 1975.

Contains many maps, charts, pictures. Small but useful.

607 R. Cleave. *The Holy Land Satellite Atlas: Student Map Manual Illustrated Supplement.* Vol. 1. Nicosia, Cyprus: Rohr Productions, 1994.

A beautifully produced collection of satellite maps as well as expert photography of the land of Israel. The pictures and maps alone are worth the price of this unique volume. Perhaps for those wanting traditional maps there are too many satellite pictures, but it is sure to hold one's attention. The data are very brief and not too helpful except in summary fashion for the student.

608 J. L. Gardner (ed.). *Reader's Digest Atlas of the Bible.* Pleasantville, N.Y./Montreal: Reader's Digest Association, 1981.

A moderately sized atlas with carefully constructed maps that show movement of the ancient Israelites and also the Christian community. Illustrations, reconstructions, and charts are expertly done and useful. The scholars with significant input include D. N. Freedman, G. MacRae, M. Tanenbaum, as well as several others.

609 S. Jenkins. *Bible Mapbook.* Oxford: Lion, 1985.

A brief guide to the events of the Bible with well-illustrated maps that show movement in the various events of both the Old and New Testaments as well as the topography of the land in many instances. Well designed and unique in its format.

610 H. G. May et al. *Oxford Bible Atlas*. New York/London: Oxford University Press, 1962. Third edition with J. Day (ed.): 1984.

Small but useful for beginners.

611 J. H. Negenman. *New Atlas of the Bible*. Edited by H. H. Rowley. Translated by H. Hoskins and R. Beckley. Garden City: Doubleday/London: Collins, 1969. Original title: *De bakermat van de Bijbel*. Netherlands.

Not bad for the price, but so much more is available elsewhere.

612 *Nelson's Complete Book of Bible Maps & Charts: Old and New Testament*. Nashville: Nelson, 1993.

Useful, but nothing here that would commend itself except for the lower cost of the volume. Charts are useful and maps are acceptable.

613 J. H. Paterson and D. J. Wiseman (eds.). *New Bible Atlas*. Leicester/Wheaton: InterVarsity, 1985.

Although smaller than many of the more recent atlases, this contains a useful collection of maps, diagrams, archaeologists' reconstructions, and charts of biblical events and history. Brief especially in terms of New Testament expansion of the church, but overall a valuable acquisition.

614 C. F. Pfeiffer and H. F. Vos. *The Wycliffe Historical Geography of Bible Lands*. Chicago: Moody, 1967.

Dated, but still a useful resource. The historical information needs updating, but the pictures, reconstructions, and diagrams are still quite helpful. One of the few sources that gives attention to the lands outside of Palestine.

615 J. Pritchard (ed.). *The Harper Atlas of the Bible*. New York/Cambridge/San Francisco: Harper & Row, 1987.

Arguably one of the best collections of maps and introductory material on the various places in the Bible as well as the major events and battles. Beautiful photography and helpful diagrams and archaeologists' reconstructions. An abridged form has appeared as J. Pritchard (ed.).

Harper Concise Atlas of the Bible. New York: Harper Collins, 1991.

616 C. G. Rasmussen. *Zondervan NIV Atlas of the Bible.* Grand Rapids: Zondervan, 1989.

Good historical information and useful maps. Unfortunately, under fifty pages on the New Testament.

617 J. W. Rogerson. *Atlas of the Bible.* New York/Oxford: Facts on File, 1985.

A superb Bible atlas, including newly-drawn maps, extensive helpful essays, and excellent illustrations and beautiful photography of ancient sites. Mostly of the Old Testament events and maps of Palestine and the Middle East, but also useful on the New Testament.

618 G. A. Smith. *Historical Atlas of the Holy Land.* London: Hodder and Stoughton, 1915. Second edition: 1936.

Excellently produced.

619 M. A. E. Smith (ed.). *Holman Book of Biblical Charts, Maps, and Reconstructions.* Nashville: Broadman & Holman, 1993.

A remarkably useful tool that is well designed. Some of the dates in the charts are untenable, but these are minor and do not detract from the attractiveness of the collection of maps, charts, and reconstructions. Worth the money!

620 E. Yamauchi. *Harper's World of the New Testament.* Cambridge/Philadelphia/New York: Harper & Row, 1981.

This is an excellent volume that is compact but never trivial. What is said is brief but carefully stated. The charts and reconstructions alone are worth the price, but the maps are also quite good. Historical and archaeological information is valuable.

Part 4

Introductions, Commentaries, and Canon

17

New Testament Introductions

Introductions come in all sizes, from the very brief overview to the lengthy and detailed discussion. They also cover various ranges of material, from simple recountings of the New Testament text to comprehensive treatments of canon, language, and the like. Some are designed as elementary textbooks or studybooks, while others are designed as full-scale reference tools. Each of them has a number of biases, for example, regarding whether they maximize or minimize the evidence from the New Testament, whether they emphasize a more Jewish or more Greco-Roman origin of the New Testament, and whether they place more relative emphasis upon history or theology.

Although not exhaustive, the following list of books gives the most commonly used New Testament introductions over the last 100 years, but more specifically in the current generation of biblical scholarship. There are exceptions, of course, but the student is advised to consult the more recent volumes to insure awareness of the current critical issues and of the state of the discussion. The bibliographies in these resources are often extremely helpful and warrant a regular examination. The following books represent a wide spectrum of opinions and vary in critical acumen and content. When looking for a good New Testament introduction today the student should always make sure that there is significant discussion of historical background in order to insure the proper interpretation of the New Testament literature, as well as careful documentation that allows the reader to check the sources, both primary and secondary, that have informed a writer's conclusions. It is not always the case, but generally speaking the introductions that offer a wider focus on the Jewish and Greco-Roman context of early Christianity are more valuable to the interpreter. Some introductions offer very little of this information in separate sections, but do have it in the individual treatments of the literature.

There are also very few introductions that have shown to the student why there are so many variations in the conclusions drawn from the same primary resources. In other words, it is important that attention is given not only to the historical context of the literature, but also to what the interpreter brings to the sources that leads to many of the differences of opinion among competent scholars. For example, if one's historical assumptions deny the intervention of God in history, as the resurrection of Jesus from the dead and the various miracles in the Gospels and Acts suggest, then the conclusions drawn are bound to be considerably different from those who are open to such activity. Schuyler Brown, Luke T. Johnson, and Christopher Rowland are quite helpful in this regard. On the other hand, when all things are somewhat equal in that regard, the scholar who provides more of the historical context almost invariably offers a more valuable contribution to one's understanding of the interpretation of the New Testament.

621 B. W. Bacon. *An Introduction to the New Testament.* New York/London: Macmillan, 1902.
No longer a useful tool. Outdated.

622 G. Barker, W. Lane, and R. Michaels. *The New Testament Speaks.* New York/Evanston/London: Harper & Row, 1969.
A college and seminary text that represents the best of evangelical biblical scholarship. They adopt conservative positions on the dating and authorship of the literature of the New Testament.

623 D. L. Barr. *New Testament Story: An Introduction.* Belmont, Calif.: Wadsworth, 1994. Second edition: 1995.
Basic study.

624 B. E. Beck. *Reading the New Testament Today: An Introduction to the Study of the New Testament.* Atlanta: John Knox/London: Lutterworth, 1977.

A brief nontraditional approach that focuses on the literature only discussing issues of text, canon, and source analysis. Conclusions are generally traditional, conservative, and geared to the layperson or beginning student. Author shows awareness of critical issues and interpretation. Secondary sources are dated.

625 G. Bornkamm. *The New Testament: A Guide to its Writings.* Translated by R. H. Fuller and I. Fuller. Philadelphia: Fortress, 1973. Original title: *Bibel—Das Neue Testament: Eine Einführung in seine Schriften im Rahmen der Geschichte des Urchristentums.* Stuttgart: Kreuz-Verlag, 1971.

Brief but careful introduction to the writings of the New Testament with special attention to critical methodology.

626 W. Bowman. *An Introduction to the New Testament.* Philadelphia: Westminster, 1971.

Nontechnical, geared for laypersons. Does not focus on the critical issues of New Testament literature nor does it offer a bibliography. Although not valuable from a critical stance, it nonetheless is a good first introduction for laypersons. Conclusions are traditional but informed. Questions authenticity of Pastorals, Colossians, and Ephesians, but accepts 2 Thessalonians.

627 R. C. Briggs. *Interpreting the New Testament Today.* Nashville: Abingdon, 1973. Revision of *Interpreting the Gospels.* Nashville: Abingdon, 1969.

Major emphasis on the critical disciplines for interpreting the New Testament as well as the problems that modern historiography and critical thought pose for interpretation. Careful discussion of modern problems of New Testament interpretation.

628 S. Brown. *The Origins of Christianity: A Historical Introduction to the New Testament.* Oxford Bible Series. New

York/Oxford: Oxford University Press, 1984. Revised edition: 1993.

Perceptive and well-informed description of the origins and literature of early Christianity. Focuses on the critical issues where the historian and the believer disagree in reference to early Christian faith, but also on the methodology that draws these perspectives into sharp distinction.

629 J. Carmody, D. L. Carmody, and G. A. Robbins. *Exploring the New Testament.* Englewood Cliffs, N.J.: Prentice-Hall, 1986.

A rather uniquely drafted treatment of the context and literature of the New Testament designed as an entry-level college text, yet fully aware of recent critical thought. The authors generally offer critically informed positions that tend to be suspicious of traditional views of authorship, date, and provenance.

630 D. A. Carson, D. J. Moo, and L. Morris. *An Introduction to the New Testament.* Grand Rapids: Zondervan, 1992.

Generally well informed but, like some of the classical introductions, shows little interest in the historical context (Jewish or Greco-Roman) in which the New Testament was written. Clarifies the background, date, and authorship of each book of the New Testament. Carefully written showing awareness of best resources available. Offers traditional positions that are not equally well defended.

631 E. Charpentier. *How to Read the New Testament.* Translated by J. Bowden. New York: Crossroad, 1984. Original title: *Pour lire le Nouveau Testament.* Paris: 1981.

Describes literary stages of the development of the New Testament, then focuses on context and content of New Testament writings in a chronological sequence. Awareness of critical issues, but written from an engaging nontechnical stance. French Catholic perspective and well illustrated.

632 B. S. Childs. *The New Testament as Canon: An Introduction.* London: SCM, 1984/Philadelphia: Fortress, 1985.

An unusual approach that all but ignores the historical context of the New Testament in favor of focusing on the issue of the New Testament as canon of the Church. Shows awareness of recent critical interpretation of the New Testament literature, but ignores its significance for interpretation. Childs argues that the appropriate way to read the text is within its "canonical context." He focuses on the theological meaning of the text for faith, however.

633 B. Chilton. *Beginning New Testament Study.* Grand Rapids: Eerdmans/London: SPCK, 1986.

Written for beginning students focusing on the primary message of the Gospels and Paul and the means of interpreting that message for the contemporary generation. Brief discussion of Jewish and Greco-Roman context as well as significant issues in New Testament interpretation. Easy to read, relevant, and well informed.

634 R. F. Collins. *Introduction to the New Testament.* Garden City: Doubleday, 1983.

A book unlike most introductions in that it introduces critical methodology as much as the corpora of writings. The traditional higher critical methods are discussed, as well as structuralism in a fairly informative and straightforward chapter (pp. 231–71). Author has special interest in the development of the biblical canon, but is not as helpful on the interpretation of the New Testament literature itself.

635 J. M. Court and K. M. Court. *The New Testament World.* Cambridge: Cambridge University Press, 1990.

Well-illustrated and carefully presented volume.

636 H. Conzelmann and A. Lindemann. *Interpreting the New Testament: An Introduction to the Principles and Methods of New Testament Exegesis.* Translated by S. S. Schatzmann. Peabody: Hendrickson, 1988. Original title: *Arbeitsbuch zum Neuen Testament.* Tübingen: Mohr-Siebeck, eighth edition, 1985.

Unlike most introductions, this work focuses on the interpretation methodology employed by New Testament interpreters and, along with providing an introduction to the literature of the New Testament, raises important critical questions about the identity of Jesus and the history of early Christianity. Provides a wealth of critical information and resources.

637 S. L. Davies. *The New Testament: A Contemporary Introduction*. San Francisco: Harper & Row, 1988.

Examines both the Jewish and Greco-Roman context of early Christianity and the critical issues related to Gospel sources. Paul and the Gospels receive the majority of attention and the General Epistles, Hebrews, and Revelation are barely discussed. Rejects authenticity of Pastorals, Hebrews, 2 Thessalonians, Ephesians, and Colossians.

638 W. D. Davies. *Invitation to the New Testament: A Guide to its Main Witnesses*. Garden City: Doubleday, 1965. Reprinted Sheffield: JSOT Press, 1993.

A dated but valuable nontechnical introduction to the Gospels and Paul by a competent scholar who shows special awareness of the Jewish context of early Christianity.

639 M. Dibelius. *A Fresh Approach to the New Testament and Early Christian Literature.* New York: Scribner, 1936.

Significantly dated, but of special interest for those pursuing the origins and development of form criticism.

640 J. Drane. *Introducing the New Testament.* San Francisco: Harper & Row/Oxford: Lion, 1986.

Aimed for the beginner, but capable of engaging the advanced student as well. Combines earlier works on Jesus, Paul, and the early Christians. Unique format that tells the story of Jesus and the spread of early Christianity while interacting with the sources that are employed to tell that story. Balanced, informed, and sane.

641 J. M. Efird. *The New Testament Writings: History, Literature, Interpretation.* Biblical Foundations Series. Atlanta: John Knox, 1980.

After brief historical background, the focus shifts to interpreting each book of the New Testament within its own individual context. Discusses special New Testament themes of this literature including helpful background of postapostolic period.

642 M. S. Enslin. *Christian Beginnings.* 2 vols. New York: Harper and Brothers, 1938.

Discusses the origins of the Gospel message and the literature of the New Testament. Conclusions are often radical, even for today.

643 E. J. Epp and G. W. MacRae (eds.). *The New Testament and its Modern Interpreters.* BMI. Atlanta: Scholars Press, 1989.

A collection of essays on background, interpretation, and canon of the New Testament. Many of the writers are prominent in the fields in which they have written. Despite delays in publication, they try to offer a "state of the art" description of the various disciplines and fields of New Testament research. Each writer has a lengthy bibliography of his discipline of research.

644 J. M. Ford. *Bonded with the Immortal: A Pastoral Introduction to the New Testament.* Wilmington, Del.: Michael Glazier, 1987.

A beginning level resource for lay persons. Well crafted but not as helpful in critical issues.

645 M. H. Franzmann. *The Word of the Lord Grows: An Introduction to the Origin, Purpose, and Meaning of the New Testament.* St. Louis: Concordia, 1961.

Careful introduction to the literature of the New Testament with focus on the theological message of each book.

646 E. D. Freed. *The New Testament: A Critical Introduction.* Belmont, Calif.: Wadsworth, 1986. Second edition: 1991/ London: SCM, 1994.

Typical introduction with brief focus on historical context and then a look at the literature of the New Testament. Rejects authenticity of Pastorals and questions Ephesians and Colossians. Deals responsibly with the biblical text, shows awareness of current critical thought, and is written as a college text without heavy technical jargon.

647 R. H. Fuller. *A Critical Introduction to the New Testament.* Studies in Theology. London: Duckworth, 1966. Second edition: 1971.

A literary-historical critical approach to the New Testament that is balanced and fair, representing many of the current issues in New Testament scholarship, such as priority of Mark, existence of Q, pseudonymity in the New Testament (Pastorals, but also questions 2 Thessalonians and Ephesians). A compact and valuable resource that needs updating in bibliography and in recent developments in Gospels research.

648 E. J. Goodspeed. *An Introduction to the New Testament.* Chicago: University of Chicago Press, 1937.

Dated but still useful for history of interpretation. Interesting focus on the origins and circulation of Paul's letters.

649 P. Grant. *Reading the New Testament.* London: Macmillan, 1989.

Interesting, but nothing new or compelling.

650 R. M. Grant. *A Historical Introduction to the New Testament.* New York: Harper & Row/London: Collins, 1963. Reprinted London: Collins, 1971/New York: Simon & Schuster, 1972.

Strong focus on canon and the historical as proper context for understanding the New Testament. Much of the book is outdated, but still a valuable resource.

651 R. H. Gundry. *A Survey of the New Testament.* Grand Rapids: Zondervan/Exeter: Paternoster, 1970. Third edition: 1994.

Carefully written, balanced, and a helpful survey of New Testament literature. Geared as a college text and less focused on the Jewish and Greco-Roman historical context.

652 D. Guthrie. *New Testament Introduction.* Downers Grove/Leicester: InterVarsity, third edition, 1970. First edition in three separate volumes: 1961–65. Fourth edition: Downers Grove/Leicester: InterVarsity, 1990.

Discerning, massive, and comprehensive, but also traditional in conclusions. Perhaps more than the average reader has time to absorb. Favors Markan priority and the existence of a sayings source that informed both Matthew and Mark. Careful attention to details. It does not ignore the tough issues. A useful resource, but too massive for textbook use in courses.

653 E. F. Harrison. *Introduction to the New Testament.* Grand Rapids: Eerdmans, 1964/London: Pickering & Inglis, 1966. Second edition: Grand Rapids: Eerdmans, 1971.

Valuable information and carefully written by a master, but out of date. A conservative resource that argues for traditional positions on dates and authorship. Useful background information.

654 E. Hoskyns and N. Davey. *The Riddle of the New Testament.* London: Faber and Faber, 1931. Third edition: 1947.

Although no longer of value for background and introductory purposes, the writers raise the still important question of how Jesus the proclaimer became the proclaimed in the early Church.

655 A. M. Hunter. *Introducing the New Testament.* London: SCM, 1945. Third edition: London: SCM/Philadelphia: Westminster, 1972.

Easily read and well-organized introduction to the New Testament for students and laypersons. Traditional interpretations are dated, but still a helpful resource for those beginning New Testament studies. Deals with language, textual criticism, and critical analysis in an easy to understand fashion.

656 L. T. Johnson. *The Writings of the New Testament: An Interpretation.* Philadelphia: Fortress/London: SCM, 1986.

A responsible discussion of the historical and critical issues of New Testament interpretation as well as its theological dimension. Although a careful historian, he does not believe that the historian as historian can account for the phenomena of the New Testament writings. He deals carefully with the faith issues that are beyond the historian's inquiry.

657 A. Jülicher. *An Introduction to the New Testament.* Translated by J. Ward. London: Smith, Elder, 1904. Original title:

Einleitung in das Neue Testament. Tübingen: Mohr, 1894.
Second edition: 1901.

Seriously dated, but helpful for the history of interpretation and ancient sources.

658 H. C. Kee. *Understanding the New Testament.* Englewood
Cliffs, N.J.: Prentice-Hall, fourth edition, 1983. First edition
with F. W. Young: 1957. British edition: *The Living World of
the New Testament.* London: Darton, Longman & Todd,
1960. Fifth edition by Prentice-Hall: 1993.

Carefully describes the historical context of early Christianity and gives special attention to the origin and understanding of the New Testament literature with reference to primary and secondary literature. Especially
valuable in Gospel introduction and interpretation and in
the social context of early Christianity.

659 J. F. Kelly. *Why Is There a New Testament?* Background
Books 5. Wilmington, Del.: Michael Glazier, 1986.

Describes the literature of the New Testament and how
it came to be acknowledged as canon. A discussion of the
use and acceptance of Apocryphal books is also included.
Includes a helpful discussion of textual criticism, versions of the New Testament, and an interesting examination of spirituality and art in early Christianity from a
Catholic perspective. Not helpful in terms of social context, but its unique focus is a good contribution.

660 A. F. J. Klijn. *Introduction to the New Testament.* Translated by M. van der Vathorst-Smit. Leiden: Brill, 1980. Original title: *De Wordingsgeschiedenis van het Nieuwe Testament.* Utrecht/Antwerp: Het Spectrum, 1965.

Brief but capable discussion of primary New Testament
issues. Generally traditional in conclusions.

661 H. Koester. *Introduction to the New Testament.* I. *History,
Culture, and Religion of the Hellenistic Age.* II. *History and
Literature of Early Christianity.* Hermeneia FF. Philadelphia: Fortress, 1982. Original title: *Einführung in das Neue
Testament.* Berlin/New York: de Gruyter, 1980. Revised
edition: 1994–95.

This has become a standard in New Testament introduction, after which all such introductions have had to take more seriously the Greco-Roman context of early Christianity. There is considerably less attention given to the Jewish context, but the research available is foundational for inquiry into the origins and development of early Christianity and its sacred Scriptures.

662 W. G. Kümmel. *Introduction to the New Testament.* Translated by H. C. Kee. Nashville: Abingdon/London: SCM, 1975. Original title: P. Feine and J. Behm. *Einleitung in das Neue Testament.* Revised by W. G. Kümmel. Heidelberg: Quelle & Meyer, seventeenth edition, 1973.

For many years this was the standard New Testament introduction. The most recent 1975 edition has significant updates on the critical advances made since its first edition. Still relevant and represents the best of German critical scholarship. It is dated in several areas, but still quite useful and presents balanced critical positions on introductory matters.

663 K. and S. Lake. *An Introduction to the New Testament.* London: Christophers, 1938.

664 H. Lietzmann. *The Beginnings of the Christian Church.* Translated by B. L. Woolf. London: Nicholson and Watson, 1937. Third edition: London: Lutterworth, 1953. Original title: *Geschichte der alten Kirche.* Vol. 1. Berlin/Leipzig: Teubner, 1932. Reprinted as volume 1 part 1 in H. Lietzmann, *A History of the Early Church.* 2 vols. Cambridge: J. Clarke, 1993.

An informative introduction to the world surrounding the New Testament. Lietzmann, who was an accomplished linguist, sets a firm foundation in events preceding the first century and carries his story on into the early church, discussing Ignatius, Marcion, and gnosticism, among other people and topics.

665 E. Lohse. *The First Christians: Their Beginnings, Writings, and Beliefs.* Translated by M. E. Boring. Philadelphia: Fortress, 1983. Original title: *Die Urkunde der Christen: Was steht im Neuen Testament?* Stuttgart: Kreuz, 1979.

Competent even if dated in some areas.

666 E. Lohse. *The New Testament Environment.* Translated by J. E. Steely. Nashville: Abingdon/London: SCM, 1976. Original title: *Umwelt des Neuen Testaments.* Göttingen: Vandenhoeck & Ruprecht, second edition, 1974.

An excellent historical resource on the context of early Christianity even if somewhat dated.

667 E. Lohse. *The Formation of the New Testament.* Translated by M. E. Boring. Nashville: Abingdon, 1981. Original title: *Die Entstehung Des Neuen Testaments.* Stuttgart: Kohlhammer, third edition, 1972.

Begins with a focus on the New Testament canon and discusses the origins of the New Testament writings themselves beginning with the oral preaching and teaching and early Christian compositions. Offers a survey of Paul's letters, the Deutero-Pauline letters, the Synoptic Gospels, John, the other letters, and Revelation and concludes with a discussion of the text of the New Testament. With careful discussions of critical issues it stands in the mainstream of German scholarship.

668 J. G. Machen. *The New Testament: An Introduction to its Literature and History.* Edited by J. C. Cook. Edinburgh: Banner of Truth Trust, 1976.

A simple introduction geared for the beginning student and defending traditional positions about the formation of the New Testament. Significantly outdated but important in understanding the theological issues of its day.

669 L. M. McDonald and S. E. Porter. *Early Christianity and its Sacred Literature.* Peabody: Hendrickson, 1996.

Historical approach to origins of the New Testament with special focus on methodology for interpreting the New Testament and the primary events that gave rise to early Christian faith. Emphasis on the critical skills for interpretation. Introductory information about specific books is less detailed and aimed at a wider audience. Concludes with an examination of the New Testament canon.

670 A. H. McNeile. *An Introduction to the Study of the New Testament.* Oxford: Clarendon, 1927. Second edition revised by C. S. C. Williams: 1953.

Seriously dated but well written resource. Valuable for history of interpretation.

671 R. P. Martin. *New Testament Foundations.* I. *The Four Gospels.* II. *The Acts, the Letters, the Apocalypse.* Grand Rapids: Eerdmans/Exeter: Paternoster, 1975, 1978. Reprinted with corrections: 1987, 1988.

Informed of current issues and shows the value of a critical understanding of the New Testament for evangelical students. At times overly detailed without adequate explanation for beginning students (e.g., textual criticism), but contains helpful information for students. In need of a glossary, but has a wealth of valuable information.

672 W. Marxsen. *The New Testament as the Church's Book.* Translated by J. E. Mignard. Philadelphia: Fortress, 1972. Original title: *Das Neue Testament als Buch der Kirche.* Gütersloh: Mohn, 1966.

Discusses how the New Testament can be examined critically and still be the Church's book that leads to faith in Jesus Christ. Deals with historical interpretation from existentialist perspective.

673 W. Marxsen. *Introduction to the New Testament: An Approach to its Problems.* Translated by G. Buswell. Philadelphia: Fortress, 1968. Original title: *Einleitung in das Neue Testament.* Gütersloh: Mohn, 1964.

Shows an awareness of the critical positions of contemporary German scholarship and holds a generally negative stance on the apostolic authorship of most of the writings of the New Testament. Not much focus on the historical context of the New Testament as a whole, but well aware of the Greco-Roman context of most of the epistles and Gospels. Raises excellent questions about the New Testament canon at the conclusion. Is somewhat dated, but still quite useful and challenging to the conservative student.

674 B. M. Metzger. *The New Testament: Its Background, Growth, and Content.* Nashville: Abingdon, 1965. Revised edition: 1983.

Traditional and very informative with short but helpful introductions to the literature of the New Testament. Written clearly enough for the beginning and advanced student. Simple format and careful understanding by a master scholar.

675 G. Milligan. *The New Testament Documents: Their Origin and Early History.* London: Macmillan, 1913.

One of the first to bring the results of the then recent discoveries regarding the papyri to bear on questions of New Testament study. There is a large discussion of the language of the New Testament, as well as substantial treatment of the growth and development of canon.

676 J. Moffatt. *An Introduction to the Literature of the New Testament.* Edinburgh: T. & T. Clark, 1911. Third edition: 1918.

Still valuable as history of New Testament interpretation.

677 C. H. Morgan. *The Layperson's Introduction to the New Testament.* Valley Forge, Penn.: Judson Press, 1968. Revised edition: 1991.

A basic presentation of the message of the New Testament along with introductions and outlines of the various books of the New Testament. It is geared for the beginner and displays a conservative approach.

678 C. F. D. Moule. *The Birth of the New Testament.* San Francisco: Harper & Row/London: A. & C. Black, 1962. Third edition: England 1981, U.S.A. 1982.

Carefully written examination of the background of New Testament writings as well as the processes by which the New Testament came into existence as the Church's Scriptures. Not the usual introduction in format, but carefully written, insightful, and rewarding even though outdated in some sections.

679 P. Perkins. *Reading the New Testament: An Introduction.* Mahwah, N.J.: Paulist/London: Geoffrey Chapman, 1978. Revised edition: 1988.

After dealing with backgrounds, Perkins provides an investigation of the New Testament in canonical order, appreciating literary, theological, and historical dimensions. Carefully interprets critical issues for the beginner. Excellent introductory text.

680 N. Perrin. *The New Testament an Introduction: Proclamation and Parenesis, Myth and History.* New York/San Diego: Harcourt, Brace, Jovanovich, 1974. Second edition by D. C. Duling: 1982.

This revised volume maintains a clear expression of the fairly radical critical perspective of the late N. Perrin while continuing to develop the introduction to reflect more recent critical thought, asserting that this probably reflects the way in which Perrin would have moved. Perrin's late emphasis was upon metaphor and myth, and this is clearly seen in the volume.

681 J. L. Price. *Interpreting the New Testament.* New York/Chicago/San Francisco: Holt, Rinehart, & Winston, 1961. Second edition: 1971.

Introduces reader to the critical disciplines needed for modern biblical inquiry, then applies these disciplines to the New Testament literature. Accepts the priority of Mark, the presence of pseudepigraphy in the New Testament, and has a helpful discussion of the context of the postapostolic writings in the New Testament.

682 C. B. Puskas. *Introduction to the New Testament.* Peabody: Hendrickson, 1989.

A brief introduction that discusses a number of the background issues of New Testament study. Apart from a discussion of the historical methodology and assumptions employed by critical scholars, there is little new or significant apart from mainstream conclusions regarding the usual questions of introduction.

683 J. A. T. Robinson. *Redating the New Testament.* Philadelphia: Westminster/London: SCM, 1976.

Robinson defies all convention and argues that all of the New Testament was written before A.D. 70. He has failed to convince the vast majority, but his arguments are always worth considering, since they compel the reader to re-examine presuppositions.

684 A. Robert and A. Feuillet. *Introduction to the New Testament.* Translated by P. W. Skehan et al. New York: Desclee, 1965. Original title: *Introduction a la Bible.* II. *Nouveau Testament.* Tournai, Belgium: Desclee, 1959.

French Roman Catholic perspective but Jewish emphasis. Not much that is new, innovative, or shocking here.

685 C. Rowland. *Christian Origins: From Messianic Movement to Christian Religion.* Minneapolis: Augsburg, 1985. British edition: *Christian Origins: An Account of the Setting and Character of the Most Important Messianic Sect of Judaism.* London: SPCK, 1985.

For Rowland, Jewish life and thought were clearly the mother of Christianity, especially apocalyptic ideas that he sees as so important at that time. This is not to be seen as the mother of all introductions. It is rather uneven, better when dealing with eschatology and the like.

686 S. Sandmel. *The First Christian Century in Judaism and Christianity.* New York: Oxford University Press, 1969.

Dated treatment, but one of few responsible treatments of Christianity by a Jewish scholar, especially one who was not inclined to be gullible but appreciated the tensions between the two.

687 S. Sandmel. *A Jewish Understanding of the New Testament.* Cincinnati: Hebrew Union College Press, 1957.

Attempts to make the New Testament understandable to Jews. As far as actual description and analysis of the New Testament is concerned, the work is pretty thin.

688 E. Schweizer. *A Theological Introduction to the New Testament.* Translated by O. C. Dean, Jr. Nashville: Abingdon, 1991/London: SPCK, 1992. Original title: *Theologische Einleitung in das Neue Testament.* Göttingen: Vandenhoeck & Ruprecht, 1989.

A very brief center-of-the-road introduction to the books of the New Testament, focusing upon theological orientation rather than merely more traditional questions of introduction. A bit too brief to do much good in either category.

689 E. F. Scott. *The First Age of Christianity*. London: George Allen & Unwin, 1926.

A book that attempts to combine history, literature, and theology. The result is a narrative account of much of the origin of Christianity. The critical position is a fairly moderate one, although there is a lack of strong argumentation and documentation.

690 R. A. Spivey and D. M. Smith, Jr. *Anatomy of the New Testament: A Guide to its Structure and Meaning*. New York: Macmillan/London: Collier Macmillan, 1969. Fourth edition: 1989.

The traditional questions of introduction are handled in summary fashion so that the emphasis is on the content of the New Testament. There is a large section on the world of the New Testament. Authors deal favorably with the New Testament miracles and especially the Easter event, offering a critical approach with traditional conclusions.

691 M. C. Tenney. *New Testament Survey*. Revised by W. M. Dunnett. Grand Rapids: Eerdmans/Leicester: InterVarsity, 1953. Revised edition: 1985.

Emphasis upon backgrounds, but very conservative. The Gospels are seen as records of the life of Christ and Acts as a record of the early church.

692 B. B. Trawick. *The Bible as Literature: The New Testament*. Barnes & Noble Outline Series. New York/San Francisco: Harper & Row, 1964. Second edition: 1968.

Although brief, a balanced and sane introduction for laypersons offering summaries of the historical background and understanding of the books of the New Testament.

693 H. C. Thiessen. *Introduction to the New Testament*. Grand Rapids: Eerdmans, 1943.

Seriously dated and not helpful in dealing with primary or current issues of New Testament study. Emphasis is on apologetic for traditionally conservative positions.

694 J. B. Tyson. *The New Testament and Early Christianity.* London/New York: Macmillan, 1984.

Besides a critical examination of the New Testament literature, focus is on both the Jewish and Greco-Roman context of early Christianity as well as early Catholic Christianity (ca. A.D. 75–200). Shows familiarity with recent scholarly conclusions in all areas.

695 W. C. van Unnik. *The New Testament: Its History and Message.* Translated by H. H. Hoskins. New York: Harper & Row, 1962/London: Collins, 1964.

Concise volume by one who understood both the Jewish and Greco-Roman origins of Christianity. Avoids most critical discussion, so best used as a survey for beginners.

696 A. Wikenhauser. *New Testament Introduction.* Translated by J. Cunningham. New York: Herder & Herder/Edinburgh/London: Nelson, 1958. Original title: with J. Schmid. *Einleitung in das Neue Testament.* Freiburg: Herder, 1958. Sixth revised edition: Freiburg/Vienna: Herder, 1973.

Offers traditional German Roman Catholic perspective on questions of introduction. Despite the length, it is concisely written and comes to the heart of an issue quickly. The conclusions are generally conservative regarding authorship. Significant discussion of canon issues.

697 T. B. Zahn. *Introduction to the New Testament.* 3 vols. Translated by J. M. Trout et al. Edited by M. W. Jacobus. New York: Scribners/Edinburgh: T. & T. Clark, 1909. Original title: *Einleitung in das Neue Testament.* 2 vols. Leipzig: Deichert, 1897, 1899.

An enduring conservative German introduction that went against the wave created by F. C. Baur (e.g., discussion begins with the epistle of James). The surveys of earlier research are still valuable and some of the discussions though dated still rate among the best to be found in an introduction.

18

Synopses

18.1 Gospels

698 K. Aland. *Synopsis Quattuor Evangeliorum.* Stuttgart: Deutsche Bibelstiftung, 1964. Thirteenth edition: 1985.
Standard Greek-text edition. Full apparatus.

699 K. Aland. *Synopsis of the Four Gospels: Greek-English Edition of the Synopsis Quattuor Evangeliorum.* Stuttgart: United Bible Societies, 1972. Sixth edition: 1983.
Greek and English edition, with less complete apparatus than no. 698.

700 R. W. Funk. *New Gospel Parallels.* Vol. 1, 2 *Mark.* Sonoma, Calif.: Polebridge, 1990.

701 R. W. Funk. *New Gospel Parallels.* Vol. 2 *John and the Other Gospels.* Philadelphia: Fortress, 1985.

702 A. Huck and H. Greeven. *Synopse der drei ersten Evangelien: Synopsis of the First Three Gospels.* Translated by F. L. Cross. Tübingen: Mohr-Siebeck, 1892. Thirteenth edition: 1981.

703 J. B. Orchard. *A Synopsis of the Four Gospels in Greek Arranged according to the Two-Gospel Hypothesis.* Macon, Ga.: Mercer University Press/Edinburgh: T. & T. Clark, 1983.

704 M. de Solages. *A Greek Synopsis of the Gospels: A New Way of Solving the Synoptic Problem.* Translated by J. Baissus. Leiden: Brill/Toulouse: Institut Catholique, 1959.

A mathematical attempt to calculate the synoptic problem. Unfortunately, the Gospel authors were not writing a mathematics textbook. Arguments are intricate but unconvincing.

705 H. F. D. Sparks. *A Synopsis of the Gospels.* 2 vols. London: A. & C. Black, 1970. Earlier edition of vol. 1: 1964.

706 W. A. Stevens and E. D. W. Burton. *A Harmony of the Gospels for Historical Study.* New York: International Committee of YMCA. Third edition: 1905.

18.2 Paul

707 F. O. Francis and J. P. Sampley. *Pauline Parallels.* Philadelphia: Fortress, 1975. Second edition: 1984.

A useful reference book, in which what the editors see as parallel Pauline texts are displayed.

19

The Gospels: Critical Studies

708 S. Freyne. *Galilee, Jesus, and the Gospels: Literary Approaches and Historical Investigations.* Philadelphia: Fortress/Dublin: Gill and Macmillan, 1988.

Shows how Jesus' identity with Galilee is historically relevant to the theological understanding of the Gospels. Excellent information on the social context of Jesus and his earliest followers.

709 J. E. Goehring, C. W. Hedrick, J. T. Sanders, and H. D. Betz (eds.). *Gospel Origins and Christian Beginnings: Essays Honoring J. M. Robinson.* 2 vols. Sonoma, Calif.: Polebridge, 1990.

Includes a collection of essays examining the origins of Q as well as noncanonical literature and its relation to the canonical New Testament texts. Not all of the essays are convincing, but most are stimulating and those by Betz, Koester, and Hedrick are well worth noting.

710 J. B. Green and S. McKnight (eds.). *Dictionary of Jesus and the Gospels.* Downers Grove/Leicester: InterVarsity, 1992.

A collection of carefully written articles on Jesus and the Gospel tradition favoring a more conservative interpretation of the New Testament writings. Worth the price.

711 H. Koester. *Ancient Christian Gospels: Their History and Development.* Philadelphia: Trinity Press International/ London: SCM, 1990.

By far the best of the recent treatments available on the origins, forms, sources, history of development, and interpretation of the canonical Gospels. There is also a critical examination of ancient noncanonical sayings of Jesus, the Agrapha.

712 R. J. Miller (ed.). *The Complete Gospels.* Sonoma, Calif.: Polebridge, 1992.

A collection of canonical and noncanonical texts with introductions. The translation used is the new Scholars Version and several useful notations are found. Some of the assumptions behind the text are more fanciful than accurate, especially in dating and pointing to the reliability of the documents as sources for understanding the historical Jesus.

713 D. J. Neville. *Arguments from Order in Synoptic Source Criticism.* Macon, Ga.: Mercer University Press, 1994.

A careful description of the history of the synoptic problem as well as how the sequence of the Gospel pericopes helps clarify the synoptic problem of source and dependence.

714 G. N. Stanton. *The Gospels and Jesus.* OBS. New York/Oxford: Oxford University Press, 1989.

Answers questions from a study of the canonical Gospels on the identity of Jesus and his significance for Christian faith. Special attention given to methods of interpreting the Gospels. Useful as a text for beginning and advanced students.

715 G. Theissen. *The Gospels in Context: Social and Political History in the Synoptic Tradition.* Translated by L. M. Maloney. Minneapolis: Fortress, 1991/Edinburgh: T. & T. Clark, 1992. Original title: *Lokalkolorit und Zeitgeschichte in den Evangelien.* NTOA 8. Freiburg, Switzerland: Universitätsverlag, 1989.

A reconstruction of the social and political contexts that are reflected in the Synoptic Gospels. A major contribution that advances the issues far beyond where Bultmann had taken them in his similar work (*The History of the Synoptic Tradition*. Translated by J. Marsh. Oxford: Blackwell, 1967).

20

Commentaries

Commentaries continue to be written at an outlandish pace. Although small and relatively insubstantial commentaries continue to be produced, the tendency is for commentators to want to display their learning in great bulk and multiple volumes. Size is not to be equated with quality. Although the individual volumes in this series should be consulted for more detailed treatment, here is provided a list of three or more commentaries for each writer to provide a starting point for subsequent research. At least one Greek- and one English-based commentary is provided for each book and one can also find the old standard reference points, or the classics, which show the state of the art from an earlier perspective. These are still useful in the history of interpretation.

20.1 Synoptic Gospels

The following commentaries are only a sample of some of the best from a critical perspective. More popular texts that are also quite useful for the pastor (Barclay's commentaries, Communicators Commentary, etc.) are not listed below, but are easily found in most bookstores and libraries. A few of the selected commentaries are dated, but still stand as the classics in the field and are pivotal in the history of interpreting the particular text.

20.1.1 Matthew

716 W. D. Davies and D. C. Allison, Jr. *A Critical and Exegetical Commentary on the Gospel according to Saint Matthew.* 2 vols. ICC. Edinburgh: T. & T. Clark, 1988, 1991. Vol. 3 is forthcoming.

Arguably the best available commentaries on the background and interpretation of Matthew. Not as useful for pastors and laypersons, but place of priority goes to this volume for its critical analysis and care for detail.

717 R. Gundry. *Matthew: A Commentary on his Literary and Theological Art.* Grand Rapids: Eerdmans, 1982. Second edition: *Matthew: A Commentary on his Handbook for a Mixed Church under Persecution,*1994.

A valuable interpretation by a conservative scholar using the redactional approach with care. A significant contribution. Not all of his conclusions are warranted, but his argumentation and support are responsible.

718 D. A. Hagner. *Matthew 1–13.* WBC 33A. Dallas: Word, 1993. *Matthew 14–28.* WBC 33B. Vol. 2, 1995.

Makes a significant contribution to the interpretation of Matthew. Argues for critical positions from a conservative tradition. Quite useful interpretation of the Sermon on the Mount and the introductory material is both expansive and helpful. Volume 2 is especially worth the price.

719 D. Hill. *The Gospel of Matthew.* NCB. Grand Rapids: Eerdmans/London: Marshall, Morgan, & Scott, 1972.

Usable commentary on the English text, showing knowledge of useful scholarship.

720 A. H. McNeile. *The Gospel according to St. Matthew.* London: Macmillan, 1915. Reprinted: Grand Rapids: Baker, 1980.

Classic commentary on the Greek text.

20.1.2 Mark

721 H. A. Anderson. *The Gospel of Mark.* NCB. Grand Rapids: Eerdmans/London: Oliphants, 1976.

When published this was a new adventure that reinterpreted Mark along redactional lines, arguing that Mark was the first Gospel and seeking the theological intent of the author throughout the various sections of the Gospel. The introductory section needs some revision to bring it more up to date, but it is an excellent offering on the history of critical interpretation of Mark. Argues that the original Gospel ended at 16:8.

722 C. E. B. Cranfield. *The Gospel according to St. Mark.* Cambridge Greek Testament Commentary. Cambridge: Cambridge University Press, 1959. Reprinted 1979.

Especially useful on the Greek text.

723 R. A. Guelich. *Mark 1–8:26.* WBC 34A. Dallas: Word, 1989. The completion of the commentary, vol. 34B by C. A. Evans, is forthcoming.

An excellent addition to the series. Argues for Markan priority and dates it A.D. 67–69. Shows keen familiarity with German contributions to the study of Mark and gives a sane and balanced interpretation. Introductory sections are not as helpful.

724 R. H. Gundry. *Mark: A Commentary on His Apology for the Cross.* Grand Rapids: Eerdmans, 1993.

The most significant commentary on Mark to appear in years and without question the largest ever produced. This has several interesting if not strange conclusions (Mark 13–14), but by and large has become one of the standard texts on Mark. Introductory and background information is impressive and the additional special studies add to this valuable contribution.

725 W. L. Lane. *The Gospel according to Mark.* NICNT. Grand Rapids: Eerdmans, 1974.

A dated volume that needs important revision especially in the introductory material, but still quite useful in terms of exegesis. Well documented with a host of valuable references to ancient and secondary literature. Makes use of redaction criticism as an important means of determining the understanding of Mark. Assumes Markan priority and generally but not always argues for the traditional interpretations. When published this volume marked a turning point in evangelical scholarship.

726 C. S. Mann. *Mark.* AB 27. Garden City: Doubleday, 1986.

Carefully written and valuable in resources drawn into the interpretation of the text. Questions the two source hypothesis. Generally very careful exegesis.

20.1.3 Luke

727 J. A. Fitzmyer. *The Gospel according to Luke.* 2 vols. AB 28A, B. Garden City: Doubleday, 1981, 1985.

Perhaps the best overall commentary on Luke. Especially valuable in the wealth of information, footnotes, and awareness of the context of early Christianity.

728 I. H. Marshall. *The Gospel of Luke.* NIGTC. Grand Rapids: Eerdmans/Exeter: Paternoster, 1978.

An excellent resource on the Greek text of Luke that scholars and students have found quite helpful. Some sections are now dated, but not sufficiently to take away from this resource.

729 J. Nolland. *Luke.* WBC 35A, B, C. Dallas: Word, 1989–93.

One of the best from the evangelical tradition that gives careful attention to details and engages numerous positions other than his own. Conclusions tend to be traditional, but not always. This should be a standard resource for years to come.

730 E. E. Ellis. *The Gospel of Luke.* NCB. London: Nelson, 1966. Revised edition: Grand Rapids: Eerdmans/London: Marshall, Morgan, & Scott, 1974.

A solid work that is especially useful to the advanced student. Scholarly interests of the Gospel take priority and the detailed notes are burdensome to the beginner but helpful to the scholar. Some sections are now dated, but still an important contribution.

731 L. T. Johnson. *Luke.* SP. Michael Glazier Book. Collegeville, Minn.: Liturgical Press, 1991.

Interprets Luke–Acts as an apologetic history of the early church and focuses on the literary artistry of Luke as well as the theology of the text. A new and fresh approach to the Gospel within the Catholic tradition. Well written and worthwhile consulting. Employs a critical methodology, but does not allow it to become the end focus.

20.2 John

732 C. K. Barrett. *The Gospel according to St. John: An Introduction with Commentary and Notes on the Greek Text.* Philadelphia: Westminster/London: SPCK, 1955. Second edition: 1978.
Standard commentary on the Greek text. A must for detailed exegesis.

733 G. R. Beasley-Murray. *John.* WBC 36. Dallas: Word, 1987.
Although not the most complete, this is certainly one of the standard works to which all serious interpreters should turn. Deals with most historical and theological issues evenhandedly and from a traditional approach.

734 J. H. Bernard. *A Critical and Exegetical Commentary on the Gospel according to St. John.* 2 vols. Edited by A. H. McNeile. ICC. Edinburgh: T. & T. Clark, 1928.
One of the fine classical commentaries that still has benefit for the scholar and advanced student. It should be used along with more recent commentaries.

735 R. Brown. *The Gospel according to John.* 2 vols. AB 29, 29A. Garden City: Doubleday, 1966, 1970/London: Geoffrey Chapman, 1971.
Perhaps the best general-purpose commentary, combining historical and theological exegesis. Written by a prominent Roman Catholic scholar.

736 R. Bultmann. *The Gospel of John: A Commentary.* Translated by G. R. Beasley-Murray, R. W. N. Hoare, and J. K. Riches. Philadelphia: Westminster/Oxford: Blackwell, 1971. Original title: *Das Evangelium des Johannes.* Göttingen: Vandenhoeck & Ruprecht, 1964.
This was a significant addition to the commentaries on John in that it was the first major attempt to interpret the Gospel within a hellenistic context and with an existentialist interpretation. Although that approach has largely been replaced, there are still treasures to mine from this important contribution. His seeking to preserve John

from having an apocalyptic focus is unconvincing (see treatment of 5:25–28) and his discussion of the eschatology of John is not persuasive.

737 B. Lindars. *The Gospel of John.* NCB. Grand Rapids: Eerdmans/London: Marshall, Morgan, & Scott, 1972.
A fine addition to the series by a careful scholar in matters of detail. Informed by the Roman Catholic tradition and aware of the critical issues of interpretation.

738 L. Morris. *The Gospel according to John.* NICNT. Grand Rapids: Eerdmans, 1971. Revised edition forthcoming.
Hefty and apologetic for traditional and conservative positions, but an in-depth treatment of texts and worth considering. Argues that chapter 21 was an additional part added to the Gospel, but written by John. His comments about the identity of the "we" in 21:24 are unconvincing, but one of the most published scholars in Johannine studies who generally accounts well for his positions.

739 R. Schnackenburg. *The Gospel according to St. John.* 3 vols. Translated by K. Smyth et al. New York: Crossroad/London: Burns & Oates, 1968–82. Original title: *Das Johannesevangelium.* Freiburg: Herder, 1965–75.
Represents the best of the Catholic tradition. Thorough, clear, and well informed. Valuable historical introduction and careful notations on primary sources and secondary ones as well.

20.3 Acts

740 C. K. Barrett. *A Critical and Exegetical Commentary on the Book of Acts 1–14.* 2 vols. ICC. Edinburgh: T. & T. Clark, 1994– .
Destined to be a standard treatment. These volumes are thorough, informative, and essential.

741 F. F. Bruce. *Commentary on the Book of Acts: The English Text with Introduction, Exposition and Notes.* NICNT. Grand Rapids: Eerdmans, 1954. Revised edition: 1988.
A standard and solid work that supports conservative views about the authorship of the book (Luke) as well as an early dating (early 60s). With recent revisions, this re-

mains a valuable resource. It is a fine supplement to his earlier and still useful commentary on the Greek text (see no. 742).

742 F. F. Bruce. *The Acts of the Apostles: The Greek Text with Introduction and Commentary.* Grand Rapids: Eerdmans/ Leicester: Tyndale, 1951. Third revised edition: Grand Rapids: Eerdmans/Leicester: InterVarsity, 1990.

A most welcome revision of an older and enduring treatment of the Greek text of Acts. This revision has made many necessary changes and now resurfaces as one of the standard texts on Acts. The introductory material has been significantly updated without changing the traditional conclusions about date, authorship, and intent.

743 H. Conzelmann. *Acts of the Apostles.* Translated by J. Limburg, A. T. Kraabel, and D. H. Juel. Hermeneia. Philadelphia: Fortress, 1987. Original title: *Die Apostelgeschichte.* Tübingen: Mohr, 1963. Revised edition: 1972.

One of the standard resources on Acts. Argues for a date of composition around A.D. 80–100. Unlike the Tübingen tradition, he rejects a second-century dating. The wealth of knowledge of the primary and secondary sources that the author brings to this volume make it exceptionally worth reading. The many *excursi* also add to the importance of this resource.

744 E. Haenchen. *The Acts of the Apostles: A Commentary.* Translated by B. Noble, G. Shinn, H. Anderson, and R. McL. Wilson. Philadelphia: Westminster/Oxford: Blackwell, 1971. Original title: *Die Apostelgeschichte.* Göttingen: Vandenhoeck & Ruprecht, fourteenth edition, 1965.

This has long been the standard commentary on Acts, showing an enormous wealth of knowledge about the history of early Christianity and its interpretation in the Apostolic Church. An essential resource for all studies of Acts and the growth of early Christianity. Based on the Greek text and awareness of vast amounts of primary and secondary literature. Essential reading for introductory matters as well.

745 L. T. Johnson. *The Acts of the Apostles.* SP. Michael Glazier Book. Collegeville, Minn.: Liturgical Press, 1992.

Careful description of the nature of this writing and its ancient genre as well as the apologetic purposes of its author. Without use of a lot of scholarly jargon, he makes use of the results of the best of critical scholarship available from German, French, and English resources, and shows special awareness of the use and interpretation of Acts in primary sources of antiquity. Unlike many commentaries on Acts, this one shows an interest in both historical interpretation and its theological aims and significance.

746 R. N. Longenecker. "Acts." Pp. 207–573 in *The Expositor's Bible Commentary* 9. Edited by F. E. Gaebelein. Grand Rapids: Zondervan/London: Hodder & Stoughton, 1981.

Surprisingly substantial evangelical treatment in a nontechnical series.

747 B. W. Winter (ed.). *The Book of Acts in its First Century Setting.* I. B. W. Winter and A. D. Clarke (eds.). *The Book of Acts in its Ancient Literary Setting.* II. D. W. J. Gill and C. Gempf (eds.). *The Book of Acts in its Graeco-Roman Setting.* III. B. Rapske. *The Book of Acts and Paul in Roman Custody.* IV. R. Bauckham (ed.). *The Book of Acts in its Palestinian Setting.* V. I. Levinskaya. *The Book of Acts in its Diaspora Setting.* VI. I. H. Marshall and D. Peterson (eds.). *The Book of Acts in its Theological Setting.* Grand Rapids: Eerdmans/ Carlisle: Paternoster, 1993–.

A useful collection of studies on various aspects of the social and historical setting of the Book of Acts. It seeks to bring an update to the old and still useful five-volume series edited by F. J. Foakes-Jackson and K. Lake. *The Beginnings of Christianity.* 5 vols. London: Macmillan, 1920–33. Reprinted: Grand Rapids: Baker, 1979. There is some fine work presented in the first four volumes, now published. Balanced, in-depth, and giving Luke his just deserves at last!

20.4 Pauline Letters

20.4.1 Romans

748 C. E. B. Cranfield. *A Critical and Exegetical Commentary on the Epistle to the Romans*. 2 vols. ICC. Edinburgh: T. & T. Clark, 1975, 1979.

Still the best in virtually every dimension, especially if supplemented by W. Sanday and A. C. Headlam's *A Critical and Exegetical Commentary on the Epistle to the Romans*. ICC. Edinburgh: T. & T. Clark, fifth edition, 1902, for a few more details on Greek.

749 J. D. G. Dunn. *Romans*. 2 vols. WBC 50. Waco: Word, 1988. Thorough bibliographies, and written from Dunn's perspective on Paul, which is between the traditional view and E. P. Sanders's position. Valuable information and interpretation not found elsewhere.

750 J. A. Fitzmyer. *Romans*. AB 33. New York: Doubleday, 1993. The emphasis is upon introduction and bibliography. Highly readable.

751 K. P. Donfried (ed.). *The Romans Debate*. Peabody: Hendrickson, 1991. Revised and expanded version of original: Minneapolis: Augsburg, 1977.

A set of very important articles that debate many of the most significant issues arising in the study of Romans, including purpose, destination, occasion, textual integrity, historical and sociological factors, rhetoric, and theology.

20.4.2 Corinthian Letters

752 C. K. Barrett. *A Commentary on the First Epistle to the Corinthians*. New York: Harper & Row/London: A. & C. Black, 1968.

In some ways perhaps still the best overall commentary on 1 Corinthians.

753 H. Conzelmann. *1 Corinthians*. Translated by J. W. Leitch. Hermeneia. Philadelphia: Fortress, 1975. Original title: *Der erste Brief an die Korinther*. MeyerK. Göttingen: Vandenhoeck & Ruprecht, eleventh edition, 1969.

Standard German commentary. Good on critical issues.

754 G. D. Fee. *The First Epistle to the Corinthians*. NICNT. Grand Rapids: Eerdmans, 1987.

Good on backgrounds and context, although Fee has a slightly unusual view of the problem at Corinth focusing upon rejection of Pauline authority, not factionalism and various other disputes.

755 V. P. Furnish. *II Corinthians*. AB 32A. Garden City: Doubleday, 1984.

Arguably the best commentary on 2 Corinthians in combining attention to the text with appreciation of the Greco-Roman background, including archaeology.

756 C. K. Barrett. *A Commentary on the Second Epistle to the Corinthians*. New York: Harper & Row/London: A. & C. Black, 1973.

In some ways perhaps still the best overall commentary on 2 Corinthians so far as readability.

757 R. Bultmann. *The Second Letter to the Corinthians*. Edited by E. Dinkler. Translated by R. A. Harrisville. Minneapolis: Augsburg, 1985. Original title: *Der zweite Brief an die Korinther*. MeyerK. Göttingen: Vandenhoeck & Ruprecht, 1976.

Bultmann at his best. Excellent attention to the Greek text, although some unique ideas on textual integrity.

20.4.3 Galatians

758 H. D. Betz. *Galatians: A Commentary on Paul's Letter to the Churches in Galatia*. Hermeneia. Philadelphia: Fortress, 1979. German translation: *Der Galaterbrief: Ein Kommentar zum Brief des Apostels Paulus an die Gemeinden in Galatien*. Translated by S. Ann. Munich: Kaiser, 1988.

Betz attempts a rhetorical approach to Galatians which has set the tenor for much subsequent research. His outline of the epistle has proved less convincing.

759 F. F. Bruce. *Commentary on Galatians*. NIGTC. Grand Rapids: Eerdmans/Exeter: Paternoster, 1982.

Good attention to the Greek text without getting hung up on theology.

760 J. D. G. Dunn. *The Epistle to the Galatians*. Peabody: Hendrickson/London: A. & C. Black, 1993.

His new perspective on Paul as seen in a commentary. Highly readable.

761 R. N. Longenecker. *Galatians*. WBC 41. Dallas: Word, 1990.

A lengthy and informative commentary on Galatians, unfortunately marred by its overemphasis of ancient rhetoric as the hermeneutical key to the book.

20.4.4 Ephesians

762 M. Barth. *Ephesians*. 2 vols. AB 34, 34A. Garden City: Doubleday, 1974.

The most detailed theological treatment. Argues for Pauline authorship.

763 A. T. Lincoln. *Ephesians*. WBC 42. Dallas: Word, 1990.

A detailed commentary on most issues. Argues against Pauline authorship.

764 J. A. Robinson. *Commentary on Ephesians*. London: Macmillan, 1903. Second edition: 1904.

Still many useful comments on the Greek text.

20.4.5 Philippians

765 G. F. Hawthorne. *Philippians*. WBC 43. Waco: Word, 1983.

Readable commentary but with more than a few odd interpretations.

766 J. B. Lightfoot. *St. Paul's Epistle to the Philippians*. London: Macmillan, 1913.

Lightfoot still has much to offer from the standpoint of Greek and backgrounds.

767 P. T. O'Brien. *The Epistle to the Philippians*. NIGTC. Grand Rapids: Eerdmans/Exeter: Paternoster, 1991.

An exhaustive commentary, with very full surveys of research. It is strange that there are still several issues treated superficially (such as rhetoric).

20.4.6 Colossians and Philemon

768 E. Lohse. *Colossians and Philemon*. Translated by W. R. Poehlmann and R. J. Karris. Hermeneia. Philadelphia: Fortress, 1971. Original title: *Die Briefe an die Kolosser und an Philemon*. MeyerK. Göttingen: Vandenhoeck & Ruprecht, fourteenth edition, 1968.

> Moderate German commentary that disputes Pauline authorship.

769 C. F. D. Moule. *The Epistles to the Colossians and to Philemon*. Cambridge Greek Testament Commentary. Cambridge: Cambridge University Press, 1957.

> Amazing amounts of useful insights, especially into the Greek text, in a small commentary.

770 P. T. O'Brien. *Colossians, Philemon*. WBC 44. Waco: Word, 1982.

> Perhaps the best overall commentary, although not a lot of independent thinking.

20.4.7 Thessalonian Letters

771 F. F. Bruce. *1 and 2 Thessalonians*. WBC 45. Waco: Word, 1982.

> Solid exposition of the text.

772 I. H. Marshall. *1 and 2 Thessalonians*. NCB. Grand Rapids: Eerdmans/London: Marshall, Morgan, & Scott, 1983.

> Highly readable commentary in the E. Best tradition, which it resembles and brings up to date.

773 C. A. Wanamaker. *Commentary on 1, 2 Thessalonians*. NIGTC. Grand Rapids: Eerdmans/Exeter: Paternoster, 1990.

> Takes rhetorical analysis perhaps too seriously. Argues that 2 Thessalonians was written before 1 Thessalonians. Detailed analysis of the text, but conclusions are unconvincing.

20.4.8 Pastoral Epistles

774 M. Dibelius and H. Conzelmann. *The Pastoral Epistles*. Translated by P. Buttolph and A. Yarboro. Hermeneia. Philadelphia: Fortress, 1972. Original title: *Die Pastoralbriefe*. Tübingen: Mohr-Siebeck, fourth edition revised by H. Conzelmann, 1955.

Standard German commentary. Takes non-Pauline authorship as a certain conclusion.

775 J. N. D. Kelly. *A Commentary on the Pastoral Epistles*. New York: Harper & Row/London: A. & C. Black, 1963.

A very readable commentary. Accepts Pauline authorship.

776 G. W. Knight III. *Commentary on the Pastoral Epistles*. NIGTC. Grand Rapids: Eerdmans/Carlisle: Paternoster, 1993.

A very full although perhaps too word-centered commentary. Argues at length for Pauline authorship.

777 J. D. Quinn. *The Letter to Titus*. AB 35. New York: Doubleday, 1990.

Full commentary on a short book, long overdue.

20.5 Hebrews and General Letters

20.5.1 Hebrews

778 H. W. Attridge. *The Epistle to the Hebrews*. Hermeneia. Minneapolis: Fortress, 1989.

Good at utilizing extrabiblical literature. Arguably the best on Hebrews.

779 W. L. Lane. *Hebrews*. 2 vols. WBC 47A, B. Dallas: Word, 1991.

Lane attempts to introduce some recent work in discourse analysis by G. H. Guthrie (*The Structure of Hebrews: A Text-Linguistic Analysis*. NovTSup 73. Leiden: Brill, 1994). This is sometimes successful but sometimes appears more like a late addition rather than a fully integrated part of the commentary.

780 F. F. Bruce. *The Epistle to the Hebrews*. NICNT. Grand Rapids: Eerdmans, 1964. Second edition: 1990.

Vintage (revised) Bruce. He pays attention to the text, unlike a good number of commentators on this book, who have their theological agendas too firmly in place.

20.5.2 James

781 P. Davids. *Commentary on James*. NIGTC. Grand Rapids: Eerdmans/Exeter: Paternoster, 1982.

Argues that the Book of James is revised homiletical material from James, the brother of Jesus.

782 M. Dibelius and H. Greeven. *James.* Translated by M. A. Williams. Hermeneia. Philadelphia: Fortress, 1976. Original title: *Der Brief des Jakobus.* Revised by H. Greeven. MeyerK. Göttingen: Vandenhoeck & Ruprecht, eleventh edition, 1964.

German commentary in virtually every way. Detailed, critical, useful for the careful scholar.

783 S. Laws. *The Epistle of James.* New York: Harper & Row/London: A. & C. Black, 1980.

Useful commentary on the English text with sympathy for Roman origins.

784 J. B. Mayor. *The Epistle of St. James.* London: Macmillan, 1897. Third edition: 1913.

Still the most attentive to the Greek text.

20.5.3 Petrine Letters and Jude

20.5.3.1 1 PETER

785 E. G. Selwyn. *The First Epistle of St. Peter.* London: Macmillan, 1946. Second edition: 1947.

Full commentary on the Greek text.

786 J. R. Michaels. *1 Peter.* WBC 49. Waco: Word, 1989.

Some odd interpretations, but generally reliable summaries and bibliographies.

787 L. Goppelt. *A Commentary on I Peter.* Edited by F. Hahn. Translated by J. E. Alsup. Grand Rapids: Eerdmans, 1993. Original title: *Der erste Petrusbrief.* MeyerK. Göttingen: Vandenhoeck & Ruprecht, 1978.

One of the first commentaries to approach the text from a sociological standpoint.

20.5.3.2 2 PETER AND JUDE

788 J. N. D. Kelly. *A Commentary on the Epistles of Peter and Jude.* New York: Harper & Row/London: A. & C. Black, 1969.

Still one of the best commentaries. Very readable.

789 R. Bauckham. *Jude, 2 Peter.* WBC 50. Waco: Word, 1983.

Argues for pseudonymous authorship of 2 Peter.

790 J. B. Mayor. *The Epistle of St. Jude and the Second Epistle of St. Peter.* London: Macmillan, 1907.
Very detailed treatment of the Greek text.

791 J. H. Neyrey. *2 Peter, Jude.* AB 37C. New York: Doubleday, 1993.
One of the first commentaries to utilize a distinctive social-science perspective, but susceptible to being reductionistic.

20.5.4 Johannine Letters

792 R. Brown. *The Epistles of John.* AB 30. Garden City: Doubleday, 1982.
A definite defense of the Johannine school, as well as a detailed commentary from a theological perspective.

793 I. H. Marshall. *The Epistles of John.* NICNT. Grand Rapids: Eerdmans, 1978.
A fine commentary in the J. R. W. Stott tradition.

794 S. S. Smalley. *1, 2, 3 John.* WBC 51. Waco: Word, 1984.
Good discussion of the Greek text.

20.6 Revelation

795 G. B. Caird. *A Commentary on the Revelation of St. John the Divine.* New York: Harper & Row/London: A. & C. Black, 1966.
Emphasis upon the apocalyptic dimensions of the book.

796 R. H. Charles. *A Critical and Exegetical Commentary on the Revelation of St. John.* 2 vols. ICC. Edinburgh: T. & T. Clark, 1920.
Classic treatment of the Greek text, with plenty of other material in the introduction and throughout regarding the religious, historical, and cultural background.

797 R. H. Mounce. *The Book of Revelation.* NICNT. Grand Rapids: Eerdmans, 1977.
Balanced treatment of prophetic and apocalyptic dimensions but attention to background as well.

21

Canon, Pseudonymity, and
Canonical Hermeneutics

The issue of canon is really two issues: the historical process by which the canon came into being and when, and the role that the canon should play in interpretation of the New Testament. In some ways it is unfortunate that they are both labeled canon criticism, since, although related, they are concerned with a number of different issues. The first is a historical enterprise by which one investigates the evidence within and without the New Testament to establish the timeframe, order, reasoning, etc., that led to the formation of the canon. The second usually involves a distinct theological element. Related to the issue of canonical formation is the question of whether pseudonymous literature is found in the New Testament, a subject of recent intense debate. A sampling of basic texts on these issues is included below. Those interested will want to consult the standard reference tools as well, such as the *Anchor Bible Dictionary* (see no. 591), *Interpreter's Bible Dictionary* (see no. 588), *TDNT* (see no. 117), *The New Testament and its Modern Interpreters* (see no. 643) and McDonald's *Formation of the Christian Biblical Canon* (no. 820).

21.1 New Testament Canonical Formation

The problems of historical reconstruction regarding canonical formation are immense. In recent discussion, one of the most

213

highly debated issues has to do with the dating of the Muratorian fragment. Those taking a second-century date generally align themselves with an early date of canonical formation and are less inclined to see much pseudonymous literature in the New Testament. Those taking a fourth-century date for this document generally align themselves with a late date of canonical formation and are more inclined to allow for pseudonymous literature in the New Testament.

798 P. Achtemeier. *The Inspiration of Scripture: Problems and Proposals.* Philadelphia: Westminster, 1980.

A helpful resource on the canon that generally takes the conservative positions of von Campenhausen.

799 P. R. Ackroyd and C. F. Evans (eds.). *The Cambridge History of the Bible.* Vol. 1. Cambridge: Cambridge University Press, 1976.

Includes a number of useful essays on canon.

800 K. Aland. *The Problem of the New Testament Canon.* Westminster, Md.: Canterbury/London: Mowbray, 1962.

A brief volume that raises important questions about the formation of the canon including reliability of a second-century dating of that formation. He is also concerned about the viability of a canon that has so much diversity.

801 J. Barr. *Holy Scripture: Canon, Authority, Criticism.* Philadelphia: Westminster/Oxford: Clarendon, 1983.

Still an important work that helps isolate the nodal problems revolving around canon issues. Asks whether and how the Jewish people were a "people of the Book" and when writings began to take on canonical significance. Helpful in both Old and New Testament canon discussions.

802 E. C. Blackman. *Marcion and his Influence.* London: SPCK, 1948.

After Harnack, this is the best introduction to Marcion, but with more sane conclusions about his impact on the formation of the canon than Harnack claimed. See A. Harnack. *Marcion: Das Evangelium vom fremden Gott.* Texte und Untersuchungen 45. Leipzig: Teubner, 1921.

803 F. F. Bruce. *The Canon of Scripture.* Downers Grove: Inter-Varsity/Glasgow: Chapter House, 1988.

Discussion of the history and development of the canon, focusing upon the Old and New Testaments. Bruce takes a fairly traditional position arguing for a second-century context for the formation of the New Testament canon that is similar to his conclusions about the early formation of the Old Testament canon. Depends heavily on the arguments in R. Beckwith's *The Old Testament Canon of the New Testament Church and its Background in Early Judaism.* Grand Rapids: Eerdmans/London: SPCK, 1985.

804 H. von Campenhausen. *The Formation of the Christian Bible.* Translated by J. A. Baker. Philadelphia: Fortress/London: A. & C. Black, 1972. Original title: *Die Entstehung der Christlichen Bibel.* Tübingen: Mohr-Siebeck, 1968.

One of the most significant texts on the formation of the canon and the one which has become the starting place for canon research. Argues that the New Testament was largely formed at the end of the second century in response to the Montanists and dates the Muratorian fragment in the late second century. Shows how the Old Testament increasingly became a book that needed a supplement for the Christian community.

805 J. H. Charlesworth. *The Old Testament Pseudepigrapha and the New Testament: Prolegomena for the Study of Christian Origins.* Cambridge: Cambridge University Press, 1985.

A valuable contribution to the study of the earliest Christian sacred Scriptures that included references to noncanonical writings. Good discussion of Jude 14.

806 P. J. Cunningham. *Exploring Scripture: How the Bible Came to Be.* New York/Mahwah, N.J.: Paulist, 1992.

Nothing new here, but a useful guide to Catholic positions.

807 J. D. G. Dunn. *Unity and Diversity in the New Testament.* Philadelphia: Westminster/London: SCM, 1977. Second edition: 1992.

Raises important questions about the need for a canon within the canon and observes that the early church canonized diversity and what that might mean for the church today. See also his *The Living Word*. Philadelphia: Fortress/London: SCM, 1987, where he discusses several important canonical questions including the problem of pseudonymity in the New Testament and the form of the text that is foundational for church dogma. He also discusses the four levels of canonical authority.

808 C. F. Evans. *Is Holy Scripture Christian?* London: SCM, 1971.

Asks the basic question regarding whether the church was right in seeing the need to canonize a collection of scriptures and call it sacred. Stimulating questions that are not easily answered in traditional ways.

809 D. Farkasfalvy. "The Early Development of the New Testament Canon." Pp. 97–160 in *The Formation of the New Testament Canon*. Edited by H. W. Attridge. New York: Paulist, 1983.

Penetrating study that is flawed at its most basic stance, namely, in inserting the notion of canon wherever an ancient author cites an earlier document. A common practice. Helpful in focusing on the primary literature, however. See also his "The Ecclesial Setting of Pseudepigraphy in Second Peter and its Role in the Formation of the Canon." *Second Century* 5 (1985–86) 3–29.

810 E. Ferguson. "Canon Muratori: Date and Provenance." Pp. 677–83 in *Studia Patristica* 18/2. Edited by E. A. Livingstone. Berlin: Akademie, 1982.

A pivotal article that sought to refute the arguments of A. C. Sundberg's (see no. 828) earlier work that tried to establish a fourth-century date for the origin of the Muratorian fragment. Claims the traditional view of a second-century origin and a western provenance are the most sensible conclusions. Several of his arguments are reasonable, but still he does not adequately answer the absence of any parallel documents in the second century or why

Wisdom shows up in a New Testament collection that is only paralleled elsewhere in the fourth century.

811 H. Y. Gamble. *The New Testament Canon: Its Making and Meaning.* GBS. Philadelphia: Fortress, 1985.

A helpful little book that asks the right questions and focuses on the important factors that led to the formation of the New Testament. In this treatment, he favors an earlier dating of the Muratorian fragment but later changes his view in his article "Canon. New Testament." Pp. 852–61 in vol. 1 of *Anchor Bible Dictionary.* Edited by D. N. Freedman. New York: Doubleday, 1992, and "The Canon of the New Testament." Pp. 201–43 in *The New Testament and its Modern Interpreters.* Edited by E. J. Epp and G. W. MacRae. Atlanta: Scholars Press, 1989.

812 R. M. Grant. *The Formation of the New Testament.* Hutchinson University Library. New York: Harper & Row, 1965.

Valuable treatment by an expert in the patristic field. His conclusions are traditional and he has a careful treatment of the primary sources.

813 D. E. Groh. "Hans von Campenhausen on Canon: Positions and Problems." *Interpretation* 28 (1974) 331–43.

One of the early question-raisers about the viability of von Campenhausen's position.

814 F. W. Grosheide (ed.). *Some Early Lists of the Books of the New Testament.* I. *Textus Minores.* Leiden: Brill, 1948.

A valuable collection of ancient lists of New Testament canons. Useful in research.

815 G. M. Hahneman. *The Muratorian Fragment and the Development of the Canon.* OTM. Oxford: Clarendon, 1992.

Hahneman cogently argues for an eastern provenance and fourth-century date of the fragment, much later than the traditional second-century date, and thus argues that the development of the canon took much longer than traditionally argued. Good summary of recent work. This has become the standard reference point for current discussions about the Muratorian fragment since Hahneman treats all of the important literature related to this document. Not all arguments are convincing, but most support his case. He lists useful collections of New Testament and Old Testament scriptures adopted in the ancient church.

816 E. R. Kalin. "The Inspired Community: A Glance at Canon History." *Concordia Theological Monthly* 42 (1971) 541–49.

Argues cogently that inspiration was not a criterion for accepting books into the biblical canon.

817 E. Käsemann. "The Canon of the New Testament and the Unity of the Church." Pp. 95–107 in *Essays on New Testament Themes.* Translated by W. J. Montague. London: SCM, 1964. American edition: Philadelphia: Fortress, 1982. Original title: "Begründet der neutestamentliche Kanon die Einheit der Kirche." *Evangelische Theologie* 11 (1951–52) 13–21. Reprinted as pp. 215–23 in E. Käsemann. *Exegetische Versuche und Besinnungen.* Vol. 1. Göttingen: Vandenhoeck & Ruprecht, second edition, 1960.

Raises the nodal problem of a diverse biblical canon causing division within the church rather than bringing unity. Suggests the dropping of fringe books in the biblical canon that divide the Christian community. See also his *Das Neue Testament als Kanon: Dokumentation und kritische Analyse zur gegenwärtgen Diskussion.* Göttingen: Vandenhoeck & Ruprecht, 1970.

818 H. Koester. "Apocryphal and Canonical Gospels." *HTR* 73 (1980) 105–30.

A foundational article that examines the Gospels that were included in the biblical canon and those that were not. Asks several of the why questions and calls for further investigation into the canonical Gospels and the legitimacy of their primacy in the New Testament canon. Should other Gospels also be considered as having an equal voice and witness to the historical Jesus? See also his *Synoptische Überlieferung bei den apostolischen Vätern.* Texte und Untersuchungen 65. Berlin: Akademie, 1957, which is still one of the best treatments on the use of the synoptic Gospels in the second-century church fathers. Many of its conclusions, however, are in Koester's more recent *Ancient Christian Gospels: Their History and Development.* Philadelphia: Trinity Press International, 1990.

819 H. Koester. "Writings and the Spirit: Authority and Politics in Ancient Christianity." *HTR* 84 (1991) 353–72.

Describes how the role of the spirit was understood in early Christianity and applied to office in the church, also how it eventually became identified with a biblical canon. An important contribution that challenges several traditional positions.

820 L. M. McDonald. *The Formation of the Christian Biblical Canon.* Nashville: Abingdon, 1988. Revised and expanded edition: Peabody: Hendrickson, 1995.

Discusses the historical development of the Old and New Testaments and concludes that the process was a long one in both cases and not completed until the fourth to the sixth centuries in the church. Follows Sundberg (no. 828) and Hahneman (no. 815) and places the Muratorian fragment in the fourth century. See also his "Canon (of Scripture)." Pp. 169–73 in *Encyclopedia of Early Christianity.* Edited by E. Ferguson. New York/London: Garland, 1990.

821 D. G. Meade. *Pseudonymity and Canon: An Investigation into the Relationship of Authorship and Authority in Jewish and Earliest Christian Tradition.* WUNT 39. Tübingen: Mohr-Siebeck, 1986/Grand Rapids: Eerdmans, 1988.

The standard work to consult on this matter, although not entirely convincing. Says the production of pseudepigraphs was not always with unethical purposes in mind in the ancient world—that is, to deceive the readers—but rather to carry out the theology of the writer in whose name the document was produced. Primary examples are Pastoral Epistles, 2 Peter.

822 B. M. Metzger. *The Canon of the New Testament: Its Origin, Development, and Significance.* Oxford: Clarendon, 1987.

Argues for an early date for the Muratorian fragment and consequently a fairly conservative view of canonical formation. Excellent survey of the issues and widespread use of primary sources. One of the best texts available on the formation of the canon and argues for a second-century date for the basic formation of a New Testament canon. Raises good questions and answers them from a traditional perspective.

823 E. W. Reuss. *History of the Canon of the Holy Scriptures in the Christian Church.* Translated by D. Hunter. Edinburgh: Gemmell, 1884. Original title: *Histoire de la Théologie Chrétienne au siècle apostolique.* Paris, second edition, 1852.

Significantly dated in some areas, but useful for a study of the history of the investigation of the canon. Examines both the Old and New Testaments and cites numerous primary texts that are still quite relevant in canon research.

824 A. G. Patzia. *The Making of the New Testament: Origin, Collection, Text and Canon.* Downers Grove, Ill.: InterVarsity Press, 1995.

Carefully written for wide audience. Good discussion of formatting of the NT canon with useful diagrams and list of canon collections. A good buy.

825 G. A. Robbins. *Peri Ton Endithekon Graphon: Eusebius and the Formation of the Christian Bible.* Ann Arbor, Mich.: Edwards, 1986.

Shows the importance Eusebius had in the formation of the New Testament canon. One of the better discussions of this subject and should be essential reading for those wishing to look more carefully at the New Testament canon.

826 J. A. Sanders. "Adaptable for Life: The Nature and Function of Canon." Pp. 531–61 in *Magnalia Dei: The Mighty Acts of God. Essays on the Bible and Archaeology in Memory of G. E. Wright.* Edited by F. L. Cross et al. Garden City: Doubleday, 1976.

Offers valuable insights on how a tradition becomes fixed in a written text and then assimilated into a fixed collection of Scriptures. Useful for understanding both Old Testament and New Testament canons. Essential reading.

827 W. Schneemelcher. "History of the New Testament Canon." Pp. 28–60 in vol. 1 of E. Hennecke (ed.). *New Testament Apocrypha.* Edited by W. Schneemelcher. Translated by R. McL. Wilson et al. 2 vols. Philadelphia: Westminster/London: Lutterworth, 1963, 1965. Second edition: Louisville: Westminster/John Knox/Cambridge: J. Clarke, 1990, 1991. Original title: *Neutestamentliche Apokryphen.* 2 vols. Tübingen: Mohr-Siebeck, 1959, 1964. Fifth edition: 1988.

Valuable introduction to the discussion of canon and the formation of the New Testament canon. Cites numerous primary texts and also several lists of ancient Scriptures.

828 A. C. Sundberg. "Canon Muratori: A Fourth-Century List." *HTR* 66 (1973) 1–41.

The foundational and pivotal argument for the fourth-century origin and date as well as an eastern provenance of the Muratorian fragment. His work has been significantly supplemented by G. M. Hahneman's *Muratorian Fragment* (see no. 815).

829 B. F. Westcott. *A General Survey of the History of the Canon of the New Testament.* New York/London: Macmillan, 1855. Seventh edition: 1896.

An excellent early discussion with much attention to detail and sources.

830 T. Zahn. *Forschungen zur Geschichte des neutestamentlichen Kanons.* 2 vols. Erlangen: Deichert, 1929.

Although considerably dated and argues traditional positions, this is still a valuable resource on the primary sources for canon research. Explains most of the critical texts that are pivotal in the canonical formation.

21.2 Pseudonymous Literature in the New Testament

There are three major issues discussed with regard to pseudonymous literature in the New Testament. The first is what is meant by the term "pseudonymous" and how this kind of literature would have been understood in the ancient world, if at all. The second is what kinds of biblical parallels might be appropriate for talking about pseudonymous literature (as opposed to anonymous literature). And the third is the issue of deception, and the implications this might have regarding a doctrine of Scripture. Many introductions to the New Testament and the introductions to the controverted books (e.g., 2 Thessalonians, Colossians, Ephesians, the Pastoral Epistles, 2 Peter) have discussions of some or all of these issues. The following sources are representative of some important recent statements.

831 K. Aland. "The Problem of Anonymity and Pseudonymity in Christian Literature of the First Two Centuries." *Journal of Theological Studies* 12 (1961) 39–49. Reprinted in *The Authorship and Integrity of the New Testament*, pp. 1–13. London: SPCK, 1965.

An important defense of the concept of pseudepigraphal literature in the early church.

832 R. Bauckham. *Jude, 2 Peter*, pp. 158–62. WBC 50. Waco: Word, 1983.

A defense of pseudonymous authorship of 2 Peter and the larger category of pseudonymous literature.

833 L. R. Donelson. *Pseudepigraphy and Ethical Argument in the Pastoral Epistles*. HUT 22. Tübingen: Mohr-Siebeck, 1986.

Confronts the problems of pseudepigraphy. One of the most straightforward and honest treatments of an issue that arouses emotions.

834 E. E. Ellis. "Pseudonymity and Canonicity of New Testament Documents." Pp. 212–24 in *Worship, Theology and Ministry in the Early Church: Essays in Honor of R. P. Martin*. Edited by M. J. Wilkins and T. Paige. JSNTSup 87. Sheffield: JSOT Press, 1992.

A challenging essay that raises logical questions regarding pseudepigraphy.

835 D. Guthrie. "The Development of the Idea of Canonical Pseudepigrapha in New Testament Criticism." *Vox Evangelica* 1 (1962) 43–59. Reprinted in *The Authorship and Integrity of the New Testament*, pp. 14–39. London: SPCK, 1965.

Disputes the validity of the concept for New Testament criticism.

836 D. Guthrie. "Appendix: An Examination of the Linguistic Argument against the Authenticity of the Pastorals." Pp. 224–40 in *The Pastoral Epistles*. Tyndale New Testament Commentaries. Grand Rapids: Eerdmans/Leicester: Inter-Varsity, 1957. Revised edition: 1990.

A direct response to statistical arguments.

837 M. Kiley. *Colossians as Pseudepigraphy* (esp. pp. 15–35). Biblical Seminar. Sheffield: JSOT Press, 1986.

A discussion of the concept of pseudonymous literature in relation to literary parallels in the ancient world.

838 G. W. Knight III. *Commentary on the Pastoral Epistles*, pp. 21–52. NIGTC. Grand Rapids: Eerdmans/Carlisle: Paternoster, 1992.

Long and detailed defense at almost every turn of Pauline authorship.

839 A. T. Lincoln. *Ephesians*, pp. lix–lxiii. WBC 42. Dallas: Word, 1990.

A defense of pseudonymous authorship, but a view that represents a change of mind from some of Lincoln's earlier writings. He recognizes the problem of deception.

840 D. G. Meade. *Pseudonymity and Canon: An Investigation into the Relationship of Authorship and Authority in Jewish and Earliest Christian Tradition.* WUNT 39. Tübingen: Mohr-Siebeck, 1986/Grand Rapids: Eerdmans, 1988.

This book attempts to establish the legitimacy of New Testament pseudonymous literature on the basis of Old Testament parallels. It is the most substantial work done on the subject and should be the point of reference for all subsequent studies, although it is not always convincing.

841 B. M. Metzger. "Literary Forgeries and Canonical Pseudepigrapha." *JBL* 91 (1972) 3–24.

Includes a discussion of various forgeries and many quite entertaining stories.

842 S. E. Porter. "Pauline Authorship and the Pastoral Epistles: Implications for Canon." *Bulletin for Biblical Research* 5 (1995) 105–23.

The Pastoral Epistles are used as a test case for pseudonymity and canon, with special attention to the issue of
deception.

843 A. van Roon. *The Authenticity of Ephesians*. NovTSup 39.
Leiden: Brill, 1974.
A lengthy defense of Pauline authorship.

21.3 Canonical Hermeneutics

There are essentially two schools of thought on canonical
hermeneutics, those who have followed B. Childs and those who
have followed J. A. Sanders. The first is heavily theologically
based, and although it claims not to denigrate the importance of
historical-critical study, in the end it resembles a kind of formal-
istic literary criticism of the final form of the text. The second
fully incorporates the historical-critical method into its analysis,
appreciating the role of the development of the text as an important part of how it arrived at its final form. Many find it indistin-
guishable from historical criticism. Several more recent introductions to New Testament interpretive method have summary
essays on canonical criticism (see Part 4, chapter 17).

844 B. S. Childs. *The New Testament as Canon: An Introduction*. London: SCM, 1984/Philadelphia: Fortress, 1985.
Childs's Old Testament canonical approach is applied to
the New Testament, in which he sees the canon as developing through a theological rather than a historical process. Bibliographies are extensive, discussions of history
of research are some of the best, but his proposal is essentially the same one repeated for every book. His writings
in this area have been extensive, including: *Biblical Theology of the Old and New Testaments: Theological Re-
flection on the Christian Bible*. London: SCM, 1992/Phil-
adelphia: Fortress, 1993; *Introduction to the Old
Testament as Scripture*. London: SCM, 1978/Philadel-
phia: Fortress, 1979. For a critique, see M. G. Brett. *Biblical Criticism in Crisis*. Cambridge: Cambridge University Press, 1991.

845 J. A. Sanders. *Canon and Community: A Guide to Canonical Criticism*. GBS. Philadelphia: Fortress, 1984.

Sanders discusses reasons for canonical criticism in terms of the development of the canon and its place in establishing a canonical hermeneutics relevant also for today. See also his *Torah and Canon.* Philadelphia: Fortress, 1972.

846 J. A. Sanders. *From Sacred Story to Sacred Text: Canon as Paradigm.* Philadelphia: Fortress, 1987.

Although a collection of mostly previously published articles focusing essentially on the Old Testament as canon (canonical hermeneutics), this is a valuable discussion of how texts become canonical and the whole notion of "canonical."

847 F. A. Spina. "Canonical Criticism: Childs Versus Sanders." Pp. 165–94 in *Interpreting God's Word for Today: An Inquiry into Hermeneutics from a Biblical Theological Perspective.* Edited by W. McCown and J. E. Massey. Anderson, Ind.: Warner Press, 1982.

Summary and assessment of the major proponents.

848 R. W. Wall and E. E. Lemcio. *The New Testament as Canon: A Reader in Canonical Criticism.* JSNTSup 76. Sheffield: JSOT Press, 1992.

This important work applies canonical criticism of the Sanders variety to actual exegesis of the New Testament. Contrary to a first impression, this is not one essay rewritten many times, although the same themes do keep being repeated. This showing of the implications of canonical criticism for exegesis is to be welcomed.

Author Index